"BODY" LANGUAGE

"BODY" LANGUAGE

Jeffrey G. Garrison

Kodansha International
Tokyo and New York

Illustrations by Taro Higuchi.

Distributed in the United States by Kodansha International/USA Ltd., 114 Fifth Avenue, New York, New York 10011. Published by Kodansha International Ltd., 17-14 Otowa 1-chome, Bunkyo-ku, Tokyo 112, and Kodansha International/USA. Copyright © 1990 by Kodansha International Ltd. All rights reserved.

First edition, 1990

Library of Congress Cataloging-in-Publication Data

Garrison, Jeffrey G., 1948-
    "Body" language / Jeffrey G. Garrison.—1st ed.
    p.   cm. — (Power Japanese series)
    Includes index.
    ISBN 4-7700-1502-X : ¥1,000. — ISBN 0-87011-955-9 (U.S.) : $6.95
    1. Japanese language—Idioms. 2. Nonverbal communication.
I. Title. II. Series.
PL645.G3 1991
495.6'82421—dc20   90-5016
                                                    CIP

CONTENTS

PREFACE

To those who wisely read the introduction to a book before thumbing through its contents, I will admit straightway that this is not a book about gestures. If that is what you wanted, and the title misled you into thinking this book was about, I apologize.

If, on the other hand, you are a student of the Japanese language who has the basics down and would like to spend a few idle moments learning some of the more colorful colloquial expressions in the Japanese language, many of which can be used in all but the most formal situations, then you may have found the book you were looking for.

"Body" Language is a collection of over two hundred and fifty common idiomatic phrases that contain some reference to a part of the human body. Each entry is followed by a literal English translation, an explanation, English equivalents, and one or more Japanese examples with possible English translations. The examples are all complete, original sentences, some short and others more lengthy, designed to show the range of usage for each expression.

In Japanese as in English, idioms about the body abound. A native speaker of Japanese may want someone to "use his head" (*atama o tsukau*) and mean exactly the same thing as a speaker of English. Or he may decide to "wash his feet" (*ashi o arau*), which in idiomatic usage is the equivalent of "wash one's hands," as in "I'm going to wash my hands of the whole deal."

On the other hand, our native speaker may use an expression that has an exact literal equivalent in English, but in fact shares no similar meaning, such as *ashi o hipparu* or *me o muku*. The former, word for word, means to "pull someone's leg," which of course, in English, is to "tease" someone. The Japanese, however, might best be translated as "hold someone back" or "be a drag on someone." Knowing that *me* means "eye" and *muku* means "peel," the student of Japanese might be tempted to interpret the second expression as "keep one's eyes peeled." No such luck. It means, rather, "to stare" or "to glare."

There are also a great many Japanese idioms evoking parts of the body that lack any such convenient English equivalent. This category of "body language" is the most common, and shows best the genius of the language. Anyone who sponges on their parents, for example, is said in Japanese to "bite their shins" (*sune o kajiru*), and a worker who has been fired or laid off is said to have had his head, or, more literally, his neck, cut off (*kubi o kiru*).

If you live in Japan and are not a hermit, hardly a day passes without seeing or hearing at least a few of the expressions included in this book. If you are studying Japanese outside of Japan, planning for the day when you can seek enlightenment in a remote Zen temple, teach English to businessmen at exorbitant hourly rates, steel body and mind in a karate *dōjō*, or master the intricacies of Japanese management, then be forewarned: everything you know is wrong. Or only marginally useful at best. We all learn that *tetsudau*, for example, means "help" and *tetsudatte kudasai*, therefore, means "please help me." And so it does. However, say you're trying to lift that new high-resolution 70-inch surround-sound TV you've just picked-ed up at Akihabara and position it in the living room, and you need a little help from a friend. Rather than *Tetsudatte kudasai*, it would sound a lot more natural if you said, *Te o kashite kureru?*, which is closer to the English "How about giving me a hand." This is exactly what this little handbook will introduce you to, all those colloquial expressions that, if used correctly, will give you confidence and show that you know a thing or two about the language.

Appropriate use of idioms such as those included here will not only win friends and influence people, but will boost self-esteem when you make contact and the listener responds as you expected him to, rather than simply cocking his head to one side and smiling indulgently.

To the User

Less a dictionary than a handbook, *"Body" Language* is organized to encourage browsing. We assume that the casual reader is less likely to refer to this book in search of the meaning of a recently heard expression than to pick one out of its pages that sounds interesting or useful and try it out on a native listener.

Each general category—arm, leg, head, etc.—begins with a brief introductory comment on the various meanings of a particular part of the body. These comments are intended to be informative rather than exhaustive.

As can be seen from the Table of Contents, the parts of the body are organized, as a rule, from head to foot, with exceptions like *chi* (blood) positioned at the end.

Individual idioms are listed under the part of the body they include. An idiom including two or more parts of the body is listed under the part which appears first in the idiom. Thus, *te mo ashi mo denai* appears under *te* and not *ashi*.

The vast majority of idioms included in this handbook consist of three elements: a part of the body, a particle, and a verb. Within each category, idioms with this composition, occasionally joined by an adjective, appear first and are listed according to the particle, in the following order: が、から、で、と、に、には、の、は、も、and を.

Idioms not fitting the part-particle-verb (adjective) pattern appear at the end in Japanese syllabic order—*a, i, u, e, o*. These idioms, if any, either do not begin with a particular part of the body or begin with a *kanji* compound. Thus, after the last regular entry in *ashi*, *ashi o mukeru*, comes *ageashi o toru*, then *ashinami o soroeru*.

The final part of an entry is a cross reference to synonymous idioms. If these are included in the handbook, the synonym is preceded by "see also" in italics. If the synonyms are not included, they are preceded by "also" in italics.

Acknowledgments

I am grateful to my colleagues at Tsuda School of Business and *Newsweek Japan* for their valuable suggestions. In addition, I would like to thank my wife, Keiko, for writing many of the illustrative examples and patiently correcting or otherwise improving those that I wrote myself or attempted to adapt from other sources. Without her help, this book would not have been possible.

"BODY"
LANGUAGE

頭 ATAMA
Head

What better place to start than at the top, which in Japanese is *atama kara*, or, literally, "from the head"? In addition to its obvious reference to a division of the body, *atama* shares many other meanings with its English equivalent, including mind, intelligence, and top or beginning. An example of which is *atama o hitsuyō to shinai shigoto*, meaning "a job that it doesn't take any smarts or brains to do."

Some idioms, such as *atama no teppen kara ashi no tsumasaki made* (from the top of one's head to the tip of one's toes), are the same both literally and figuratively in English. You can even count cattle, horses, and other large mammals like whales as you would in English, but the pronunciation of the character for *atama* changes to *tō*, so five head of horses is *go-tō no uma*.

● 頭が上がらない *Atama ga agaranai*

"Can't lift up one's head." Can't stand up to someone, be no match for someone.

あいつは女房に頭が上がらないらしい。
Aitsu wa nyōbō ni atama ga agaranai rashii.
Word is that he's no match for his wife (is henpecked). / I hear his wife wears the pants in the family.

どうして彼は社長に頭が上がらないのだろう。
Dō shite kare wa shachō ni atama ga agaranai no darō.
Why do you suppose he can't stand up to the boss?

● 頭がいい *Atama ga ii*

"One's head is good." Be smart, sharp, bright, quick.

鈴木さんは頭がいいですね。
Suzuki-san wa atama ga ii desu ne.
Suzuki's a pretty sharp (bright) guy. / Suzuki has got a head on his shoulders.

彼女は頭のいい人が好きです。
Kanojo wa atama no ii hito ga suki desu.

She goes for smart (intelligent) guys.

● 頭が痛い *Atama ga itai*

"One's head hurts." (1) Have a headache, one's head hurts. (2) Worry over something.

(1) 二日酔いで頭が痛い。
Futsuka-yoi de atama ga itai.
I've got a headache from being hung over.

(2) ローンの事を考えると頭が痛い。
Rōn no koto o kangaeru to atama ga itai.
Just thinking about that loan makes me sick.

(2) どうして頭の痛い問題ばかり起きるのだろうか。
Dō shite atama no itai mondai bakari okiru no darō ka.
Why is it that every problem has got to be such a hassle? / Why does everything have to be such a pain in the neck?

● 頭がいっぱい *Atama ga ippai*

"One's head is full." Be preoccupied, obsessed with something.

彼は来週提出する論文の事で頭がいっぱいだ。
Kare wa raishū teishutsu suru ronbun no koto de atama ga ippai da.
All he can think about is the report he has to turn in next week. / He's got a lot on his mind, what with the report he's got to turn in next week.

彼は今娘の結婚のことで頭がいっぱいです。
Kare wa ima musume no kekkon no koto de atama ga ippai desu.
He's got this thing (a bee in his bonnet) now about getting his daughter married off.

● 頭が固い *Atama ga katai*

"Have a hard head." Be stubborn, pigheaded, unreceptive to change.

彼は頭が固い。
Kare wa atama ga katai.
He is hardheaded.

年をとると頭が固くなるものだね。
Toshi o toru to atama ga kataku naru mono da ne.
I guess the older you get the more set in your ways you become.

● 頭が切れる *Atama ga kireru*

"One's head cuts." Be a quick thinker, quick on one's feet.

あの弁護士は本当に頭が切れる。
Ano bengo-shi wa hontō ni atama ga kireru.
That lawyer is really sharp. / That lawyer is really on the ball.

● 頭が下がる *Atama ga sagaru*

"One's head lowers." Admire, take one's hat off to someone.

佐々木さんの勤勉さには頭が下がる。
Sasaki-san no kinben-sa ni wa atama ga sagaru.
You've really got to hand it (take your hat off) to Sasaki for how
 hard he works.

盲導犬の忠実さに頭の下がる思いがした。
Mōdō-ken no chūjitsu-sa ni atama no sagaru omoi ga shita.
I was really impressed by how loyal Seeing Eye dogs are.

● 頭が鈍い *Atama ga nibui*

"One's head is dull." Be dull-witted, slow-witted.

こんなに説明してもわからないとは、彼はちょっと頭が鈍いの
 かな。
*Konna ni setsumei shite mo wakaranai to wa, kare wa chotto
 atama ga nibui no ka na.*
He must be a little slow (thick) if he still doesn't understand after
 all the explaining I've done.

● 頭が古い *Atama ga furui*

"One's head is old." Be behind the times, be of the old school.

お父さんは頭が古いよ。
Otōsan wa atama ga furui yo.
Oh, Dad, you're so out of it. / You're such an old fogy, Dad.

私の頭が古いのか、同棲する人達の考えは理解できない。
*Watashi no atama ga furui no ka, dōsei suru hitotachi no kangae
 wa rikai dekinai.*
Maybe I'm just old-fashioned, but I can't understand people
 who live together without being married (who shack up).

Don't be tempted to think the next idiom means anything
like its English literal equivalent. It doesn't. It's a compli-

ment in Japanese to tell someone they have a "soft head," because it means that they are someone you can talk to, someone who might even change his opinion.

● 頭が柔らかい *Atama ga yawarakai*

"One's head is soft." Be flexible, receptive to new things.

あの先生は年の割りに頭が柔らかい。
Ano sensei wa toshi no wari ni atama ga yawarakai.
That teacher is pretty open-minded for someone her age.

頭が柔らかいから子供は物覚えが早い。
Atama ga yawarakai kara kodomo wa mono-oboe ga hayai.
Kids pick up things so quickly because they are still impressionable.

● 頭が悪い *Atama ga warui*

"One's head is bad." Be dim-witted, slow, soft in the head, not playing with a full deck.

あいつは本当に頭が悪い。
Aitsu wa hontō ni atama ga warui.
That guy's so stupid! / God, he's dumb! / What a lamebrain (knucklehead)!

このコンピュータのソフトは頭が悪い。
Kono konpyūta no sofuto wa atama ga warui.
This computer software is the pits (not up to snuff).

頭の悪いやりかたをして失敗した。
Atama no warui yarikata o shite shippai shita.
I blew it because of the stupid way I tried to do things.

● 頭に来る *Atama ni kuru*

"Come to one's head." (1) Get mad, get angry. (2) Flip one's lid, flip out, freak out.

(1) 頭に来た、もう我慢できない!
Atama ni kita, mō gaman dekinai!
Boy, does that burn me up! I'm not taking it any more!

彼の横柄な態度は、全く頭に来る。
Kare no ōhei na taido wa, mattaku atama ni kuru.
His arrogance really gets me! / He acts so big, it really pisses me off.

(2) あんなかっこうをして、彼女は頭に来たんじゃないか。
Anna kakkō o shite, kanojo wa atama ni kitan ja nai ka.
She must have gone off her rocker (lost her marbles), the way she's dressed.

● 頭の回転が早い *Atama no kaiten ga hayai*

"One's head turns over fast." Smart, quick-witted, quick on the uptake.

彼女は頭の回転が早い。
Kanojo wa atama no kaiten ga hayai.
She's as smart as a whip. / She has a mind like a steel trap.

● 頭の出来が違う *Atama no deki ga chigau*

"One's head is made differently." Be (a lot) smarter than someone else.

東大出は頭の出来が違うね。
Tōdai-de wa atama no deki ga chigau ne.
University of Tokyo grads do seem to have more on the ball.

君と僕では頭の出来が違うよ。
Kimi to boku de wa atama no deki ga chigau yo.
You and I are in different leagues, friend.

● 頭を抱える *Atama o kakaeru*

"Hold one's head in one's hands." Be at a loss for an answer, don't know what to do.

むずかしい問題に皆は頭を抱えた。
Muzukashii mondai ni mina wa atama o kakaeta.
Everyone was at their wit's end trying to solve the problem. / The problem had everyone stumped (wringing their hands).

盗難事件続発に校長は頭を抱え込んだ。
Tōnan jiken zokuhatsu ni kōchō wa atama o kakaekonda.
The principal was tearing her hair out trying to figure out what to do about all the thefts that had been taking place.

● 頭を下げる *Atama o sageru*

"Lower one's head." (1) Bow to (in greeting). (2) Give in to, bow to.

(1) 彼は深々と頭を下げて挨拶した。

Kare wa fukabuka to atama o sagete aisatsu shita.
He greeted us with a deep bow.

(2) あんな奴に頭を下げて取り引きを頼む気はないね。
Anna yatsu ni atama o sagete torihiki o tanomu ki wa nai ne.
I've got no intention of kowtowing to a guy like that just to get
him to do business with us. / There's no way I'm going to go
to that guy on my hands and knees and beg him to cut a deal
with us.

● 頭を使う　*Atama o tsukau*

"Use one's head." Use one's head (for something besides a
hatrack).

ちょっと頭を使えば金もうけの道はいくらでもある。
*Chotto atama o tsukaeba kane-mōke no michi wa ikura de mo
aru.*
There are all kinds of ways to make money if you just use your
head (the old bean) a little.

頭は生きている間に使わなくっちゃ。
Atama wa ikite iru aida ni tsukawanakutcha.
I figure that as long as you are alive and kicking you should use
your head for something besides a hatrack.

● 頭を冷やす　*Atama o hiyasu*

"Cool one's head." Cool down, cool off, relax, take it easy,
calm down.

散歩でもして頭を冷やしてこよう。
Sanpo de mo shite atama o hiyashite koyō.
I think I'll take a walk and try to cool down.

頭を冷やして出直してこい。
Atama o hiyashite denaoshite koi.
Come back and give it another try when you've settled down a lit-
tle.

● 頭から　*Atama kara*

"From the head." (1) From the start. (2) Out of hand, right off.

(1) もう一度頭から歌いましょう。
Mō ichido atama kara utaimashō.
All right, let's sing it again from the top.

(2) 政府の正当性を頭から否定するむきもある。
Seifu no seitō-sei o atama kara hitei suru muki mo aru.
There are some who dispute the very notion that the government
  is legitimate at all.

● 頭でっかち *Atama dekkachi*

"Big (large) headed." (1) [Of the size of a person's head] big-
  headed, have a big head. (2) [Of an institution] top-heavy, too
  many chiefs and not enough Indians. (3) [Of a person or way
  of thinking] academic, intellectual, pointy-headed.

(1) あいつは頭でっかちだな。
Aitsu wa atama dekkachi da na.
Look at the size of that guy's head, would you.

(2) あそこは天下りの役員ばかりで、頭でっかちな会社だ。
*Asoko wa amakudari no yakuin bakari de, atama dekkachi na
  kaisha da.*
That company is top-heavy, with former government officials fill-
  ing the management ranks.

(3) 頭でっかちな意見は説得力に欠ける。
Atama dekkachi na iken wa settoku-ryoku ni kakeru.
Pointy-headed (ivory-tower) opinions are unconvincing.

髪 KAMI Hair   毛 KE Hair

Both *kami* and *ke* mean hair, but it's usually the former
you'll use when referring to human hair. *Ke* alone, although it does mean human hair, is most often used for
fur. Sometimes they're even used together, as in *Kami no
ke ga mijikai*, or "He has short hair."

  There aren't many idioms with either *kami* or *ke*. Those
included, however, are graphic, the first one depicting
what in English would be a matter of the heart.

● 後ろ髪を引かれる（思い）*Ushirogami o hikareru (omoi)*

"Feel like the hair on the back of one's head is being pulled."
  Reluctantly, with a heavy heart.

彼は後ろ髪を引かれる思いで故郷を後にした。
Kare wa ushirogami o hikareru omoi de kokyō o ato ni shita.
He left his hometown with a heavy heart.

彼女は後ろ髪を引かれる思いで年老いた母のいる家を出た。
*Kanojo wa ushirogami o hikareru omoi de toshioita haha no iru
ie o deta.*
It was hard for her to leave her old mother alone. / She almost
couldn't find it in her heart to leave her aged mother alone at
home.

● 毛の生えたような *Ke no haeta yō na*

"Like something with hair on it." Not much more than, little
more than.

マンションといってもアパートに毛の生えたようなものさ。
Manshon to itte mo apāto ni ke no haeta yō na mono sa.
They call it a condo, but it's really just a glorified apartment.

あの教授は学生に毛の生えた程度の知識しかない。
Ano kyōju wa gakusei ni ke no haeta teido no chishiki shika nai.
That prof doesn't know much more than a student. / That pro-
fessor is little more than a glorified student.

額 HITAI
Forehead

Foreheads can take a real beating in Japan. The greater the presence, the lower down you've got to go and the longer you've got to stay there. None but the very devout or contrite really slap their foreheads on the floor in a deep bow from the sitting position, but there is an expression that brings such a scene to mind, *hitai o kosuritsukeru yō ni fukaku atama o sageru*, or bow so deeply that one almost scrapes one's forehead. Fact of the matter is, if you're into the Zen thing you'll find yourself scraping the *tatami* with your forehead during the morning rituals a whole lot more than you might think necessary.

● 額を集める *Hitai o atsumeru*

"Collect foreheads." Discuss, put your heads together, compare notes, huddle.

役員全員が額を集めて話し合った。
Yakuin zen'in ga hitai o atsumete hanashiatta.
The directors all had a little powwow.

家事の分担について、家族が額を集めて相談した。
Kaji no buntan ni tsuite, kazoku ga hitai o atsumete sōdan shita.
The whole family got together to work out who was going to do what around the house.

Now here's a graphic expression that I just couldn't resist putting in to fill a little space. I suppose you could even make one of those "Does a chicken have lips?" conundrums with it, because if a cat does have a forehead, well, it's damn small. Unfortunately, the same is true of most plots of land in Japan.

● 猫の額 *Neko no hitai*

"A cat's forehead." [Of a plot of land] tiny, minuscule.

私の家には猫の額ほどの小さな庭が付いています。
Watashi no ie ni wa neko no hitai hodo no chiisa na niwa ga tsuite imasu.
My house has got a yard that's about the size of a postage stamp.

顔 KAO
Face

Though women still spend a great deal of time making it up, the younger generation of Japanese men also seem more inclined to spend time doing their faces. It hasn't quite reached the point where they go to the men's room after eating to "fix their face" or *kao o naosu*, but times are changing, and sales of men's cosmetics are sky-rocketing.

The three basic meanings of *kao*, besides the part of the body to which it refers, are influence, a look or countenance, and the all-important social concept "face."

● 顔が利く／顔を利かせる *Kao ga kiku / kao o kikaseru*

"One's face works (takes effect)." Have influence, be influential, have contacts.

流通関係に顔が利く友人を紹介しましょう。

Ryūtsū-kankei ni kao ga kiku yūjin o shōkai shimashō.

I'll introduce you to a friend of mine who has some pull in distribution circles.

どこも予約でいっぱいだったが、斎藤さんが顔を利かせて新年会の会場をとってくれた。

Doko mo yoyaku de ippai datta ga, Saitō-san ga kao o kikasete shinnen-kai no kaijō o totte kureta.

Everyplace was booked up, but Saitō pulled some strings and found us a place to hold our New Year's party.

● 顔がつぶれる／顔をつぶす *Kao ga tsubureru / kao o tsubusu*

"One's face is crushed." Lose face, have one's good name tarnished, get a black eye.

紹介した人が会社で盗みを働き、私の顔はすっかりつぶれてしまった。

Shōkai shita hito ga kaisha de nusumi o hataraki, watashi no kao wa sukkari tsuburete shimatta.

My name was sure mud when they discovered that the guy I had introduced was stealing stuff from the office.

よくも俺の顔をつぶしてくれたな。

Yoku mo ore no kao o tsubushite kureta na.

You've really seen to it that I'll never be able to hold my head up around here again, haven't you. / You really screwed things up for me, didn't you, buddy? / Thanks a lot for the black eye.

● 顔が広い *Kao ga hiroi*

"One's face is broad." Have a wide circle of acquaintances.

遠藤さんはとても顔が広い。

Endō-san wa totemo kao ga hiroi.

Mr. Endo really gets around. / That Endo sure knows a lot of people.

あなたは顔が広いそうですが、誰かよい人を紹介してもらえませんか。

Anata wa kao ga hiroi sō desu ga, dare ka yoi hito o shōkai shite moraemasen ka.

Since you seem to have so many contacts, how about introducing us to someone that you think would be good (for the job)?

Don't go running off and asking people to "lend you their face" without first making sure that they are either close friends or way, way down the social scale. It's not exactly a polite expression.

● 顔を貸す *Kao o kasu*

"Lend one's face." Go (along) with someone at their request; go to someone.

そこの喫茶店まで顔を貸してくれ。

Soko no kissaten made kao o kashite kure.

Come along to the coffee shop with me.

おい、ちょっと顔貸しな。

Oi, chotto kao kashi na.

Hey, come here a minute. / Yo, get over here.

● 顔を出す *Kao o dasu*

"Stick out one's face." (1) Show up, go to, attend, put in an appearance. (2) Visit.

(1) 先日、10年ぶりの同窓会に顔を出した。
Senjitsu, jūnen-buri no dōsō-kai ni kao o dashita.
I went to my first class reunion in ten years the other day.

(1) 彼はパーティーに顔を出してすぐ帰った。
Kare wa pātī ni kao o dashite sugu kaetta.
He put in a brief appearance at the party and then left.

(2) 時々顔を出して下さいね。
Tokidoki kao o dashite kudasai ne.
Don't make yourself scarce. / Come around and see us once in a
  while.

● 顔をつなぐ *Kao o tsunagu*

"Connect one's face." Cultivate a (business) relationship.

彼らに顔をつないでおけば、後で役に立ちますよ。
Karera ni kao o tsunaide okeba, ato de yaku ni tachimasu yo.
If we keep in touch with them, it will be of some use to us later.

顔をつなぐために、そのパーティーに出席した。
Kao o tsunagu tame ni, sono pātī ni shusseki shita.
I went to the party just to be seen. / I attended the party to main-
  tain some contacts I have.

● 浮かない顔をする／浮かぬ顔をする *Ukanai kao o suru / ukanu kao o suru*

"Make a non-floating face." Have a glum face, have a sad face.

どうしたの、浮かない顔をして。
Dō shita no, ukanai kao o shite.
Why do you have such a long face? / What's the long face all about?

彼は一日中浮かぬ顔をしていた。
Kare wa ichinichi-jū ukanu kao o shite ita.
He was down in the mouth all day long. / He was moping around all day.

● 大きな顔をする *Ōki na kao o suru*

"Have a big face." Be proud of oneself, be cocky, lord it over someone.

新人のくせに大きな顔をするんじゃない。
Shinjin no kuse ni ōki na kao o surun ja nai.
I wouldn't be acting so big if I were a new guy like you.

一度世話をしてくれたからといってそんなに大きな顔をされても困る。
Ichido sewa o shite kureta kara to itte sonna ni ōki na kao o sarete mo komaru.
Just because you helped me out once doesn't give you the right to act so high and mighty.

Also 大きい顔をする *ōkii kao o suru.*

耳 MIMI
Ear

In addition to the external ear on humans and other animals, *mimi* means the power of hearing. Relatedly, it indicates a good ear for something, as for music. *Mimi* can also refer to one of usually a pair of ear-like protuberances, such as a lug or a handle, the edge of a sheet of paper, or the crust of a piece of bread. *Mimi* may be the heel of a loaf of bread, though this usage may cause confusion due to the fact that it more commonly means the crust in general. *Mimi* appears in many compounds, one of which, *mimi-gakumon* or "ear learning," means "hearsay."

● 耳が痛い *Mimi ga itai*

"One's ears hurt." Hit a sore spot, hit where it hurts.

彼の失敗談には耳が痛かった。
Kare no shippai-dan ni wa mimi ga itakatta.
My ears really burned when I heard him talk about how he had screwed things up.

彼の話は、遅刻常習犯の私には耳が痛い。
Kare no hanashi wa, chikoku-jōshūhan no watashi ni wa mimi ga itai.
It really makes me feel guilty listening to him talk about being punctual because I'm the kind of guy who'd be late to his own funeral.

● 耳が遠い *Mimi ga tōi*

"One's ears are far away." Be hard of hearing, be deaf.

私は耳が遠いので大きな声で話してください。
Watashi wa mimi ga tōi no de ōki na koe de hanashite kudasai.
I'm a little hard of hearing, so would you mind speaking in a loud voice.

祖母は最近耳が遠くなってきたようだ。
Sobo wa saikin mimi ga tōku natte kita yō da.
I think my grandmother's starting to lose her hearing.

● 耳が早い *Mimi ga hayai*

"Have fast ears." Have one's ear to the ground.

いつも井戸端会議をしている母は隣近所のことには耳が早い。
Itsu mo idobata-kaigi o shite iru haha wa tonari-kinjo no koto ni wa mimi ga hayai.
My mom's always gossiping with the women in the neighborhood, so she's always up on the latest news (skinny).

● 耳にする *Mimi ni suru*

"Make something into an ear." Hear, get wind of, find out about.

環境問題について、よく耳にするようになった。
Kankyō-mondai ni tsuite, yoku mimi ni suru yō ni natta.
You hear about the environment all the time now.

彼の悪い噂を耳にすることが多いが事実なのだろうか。
Kare no warui uwasa o mimi ni suru koto ga ōi ga jijitsu na no darō ka.
I get wind of a lot of bad rumors about him, but I wonder if there is any truth to them.

● 耳にたこができる *Mimi ni tako ga dekiru*

"Get calluses on one's ears." Have heard about all one wants to hear of something.

その話なら耳にたこができるほど聞かされた。
Sono hanashi nara mimi ni tako ga dekiru hodo kikasareta.
I've heard that story so many times that I could tell it backwards.

車に気をつけるように毎朝言われて、耳にたこができちゃったよ。
Kuruma ni ki o tsukeru yō ni maiasa iwarete, mimi ni tako ga dekichatta yo.
I'm sick and tired of being told to watch out for cars every morning.

● 耳に入る *Mimi ni hairu*

"Go in one's ear." Hear of.

株価暴落の噂が耳に入った。
Kabuka-bōraku no uwasa ga mimi ni haitta.
I got wind of a rumor that the stock market was crashing.

彼については、悪いことばかりが私の耳に入る。
Kare ni tsuite wa, warui koto bakari ga watashi no mimi ni hairu.
Everything I ever hear about him is bad.

● 耳を疑う *Mimi o utagau*

"Doubt one's ears." Be unable to believe one's ears.

突然の別れ言葉に彼は自分の耳を疑った。
Totsuzen no wakare-kotoba ni kare wa jibun no mimi o utagatta.
He couldn't believe he was hearing her say that this was the end.

あんな乱暴な言葉が、あの人の口から出るなんて、私は思わず耳を疑った。

*Anna ranbō na kotoba ga, ano hito no kuchi kara deru nante,
  watashi wa omowazu mimi o utagatta.*
I couldn't believe my ears when I heard him using such rough
  language.

● 耳を貸す *Mimi o kasu*

"Lend an ear." Listen to, give an ear to.

くだらない噂話に耳を貸す気はない。
Kudaranai uwasabanashi ni mimi o kasu ki wa nai.
I have no intention of listening to a bunch of ridiculous gossip.

政府は消費者の不満の声に全く耳を貸さなかった。
*Seifu wa shōhi-sha no fuman no koe ni mattaku mimi o kasa-
  nakatta.*
The government turned a deaf ear to complaints from con-
  sumers.

● 耳を傾ける *Mimi o katamukeru*

"Incline one's ears." Listen to, lend an ear to.

少しは他人の意見に耳を傾けたらどうですか。
Sukoshi wa tanin no iken ni mimi o katamuketara dō desu ka.
Why don't you try paying a little attention to what other people
  have to say.

国民の声に耳を傾ける政治家こそ必要だ。
Kokumin no koe ni mimi o katamukeru seiji-ka koso hitsuyō da.
What we really need are politicians who will listen to the people.

# 眉 MAYU
Eyebrow(s), Brow(s)

Most of the following idioms have to do with what lies
behind the expression on someone's face: doubt, suspi-
cion, concern, or worry.

● 眉に唾をぬる *Mayu ni tsuba o nuru*

"Apply spit to one's eyebrows." Keep one's wits about one, be
  on one's guard, be wary, keep on one's toes.

彼のもうけ話は眉に唾をぬって聞いた方がいい。

Kare no mōke-banashi wa mayu ni tsuba o nutte kiita hō ga ii.
You'd better take what he says about making a lot of money with a grain of salt.

その話はどうもうますぎるね。眉に唾をぬった方がよさそうだ。
Sono hanashi wa dō mo umasugiru ne. Mayu ni tsuba o nutta hō ga yosasō da.
You'd better watch your step. That sounds too good to be true.

Also 眉に唾を付ける *mayu ni tsuba o tsukeru.*

● 眉をひそめる *Mayu o hisomeru*

"Narrow one's brows." Knit one's brows, furrow one's brows, frown.

車内の酔っぱらいに、みんなは眉をひそめた。
Shanai no yopparai ni, minna wa mayu o hisometa.
Everyone in the train was giving the drunk the bad eye.

彼は夜中でもボリュームを上げてロックを聞くので、近所の人は皆眉をひそめている。
Kare wa yonaka de mo boryūmu o agete rokku o kiku no de, kinjo no hito wa mina mayu o hisomete iru.
The whole neighborhood is giving him dirty looks because he listens to rock music full-blast on his stereo late at night.

Also 眉を集める *mayu o atsumeru.*

目 ME Eye　眼 ME Eye

The importance of this part of the body is indicated by the number of expressions in which it figures. By my count, well over a hundred. Those selected for inclusion here reflect the wide range of meanings carried by the word. In addition to its basic reference to the seeing eye or eyeball itself, *me* includes the power of vision as exemplified most simply in the sentences *me ga warui* or *me ga ii*, which may mean to have bad or good eyesight respectively. By extension, *me* appears in many expressions concerning judgment or insight. It can also denote appearance or the way something looks, or an experience—usually bad. Although not exemplified in any of the idioms which follow, *me* also means the grain in a piece of wood, the pips on a die, or the points formed at the intersection of lines on a *go* board. Finally, one usage that you run into all the time is as a suffix after a number forming the Japanese equivalent of an English ordinal, as in *futatsu-me no mondai* (the second problem) or *shiri kara sanban-me* (third from the end or rear).

● 目が利く *Me ga kiku*

"One's eyes work." Know how to spot something good.

彼女は、版画にはなかなか目が利く人です。
Kanojo wa, hanga ni wa nakanaka me ga kiku hito desu.
She's quite a connoisseur of woodblock prints. / She has good taste in (a good eye for) woodblock prints.

See also 目が高い *me ga takai* and 目が肥える *me ga koeru.*

● 目が肥える *Me ga koeru*

"One's eyes grow fat." Know a thing or two about something, be knowledgeable about something.

彼女は骨董品屋の娘だけあって、古いものには目が肥えている。
Kanojo wa kottōhin-ya no musume dake atte, furui mono ni wa me ga koete iru.
Since her parents run an antique shop she really has a good eye for old things.

● 目が覚める *Me ga sameru*

"One's eyes wake up." (1) Wake up. (2) Come to one's senses, be enlightened. (3) [Used in the phrase ～ような *yō na*] amazing, startling.

(1) 真夜中に大きな音がしたので目が覚めてしまった。
Ma-yonaka ni ōki na oto ga shita no de me ga samete shimatta.
A loud sound in the middle of the night woke me up.

(2) 親友の心からの忠告に、彼は目が覚めた。
Shinyū no kokoro kara no chūkoku ni, kare wa me ga sameta.

The heartfelt warning from his friend brought him to his senses (woke him up, made him see the light).

(3) 彼女は目の覚めるようなピンクのドレスを着て出かけた。

Kanojo wa me no sameru yō na pinku no doresu o kite dekaketa.

She went out wearing a startling (shocking) pink dress.

(3) 関東代表のチームは目の覚めるようなすばらしい試合をした。

Kantō-daihyō no chīmu wa me no sameru yō na subarashii shiai o shita.

The team representing the Kantō area played a spectacular game.

● 目が高い *Me ga takai*

"One's eyes are high." Know something backwards and forwards, know something inside and out.

この絵を選ぶとは、さすが(お)目が高い。

Kono e o erabu to wa, sasuga (o)me ga takai.

You certainly have a sharp eye for paintings to have chosen this one.

See also 目が利く *me ga kiku* and 目が肥える *me ga koeru.*

● 目が届く *Me ga todoku*

"One's eyes reach." Keep an eye on something.

1 クラス40人に教師が 1 人では、なかなか生徒全員に目が届かない。

Hito-kurasu yonjū-nin ni kyōshi ga hitori de wa, nakanaka seito zen'in ni me ga todokanai.

With 40 students, it's pretty hard for one teacher to keep an eye on all of them.

監督の目が届かないところでさぼったりしないように。

Kantoku no me ga todokanai tokoro de sabottari shinai yō ni.

No goofing off when the manager's not watching.

● 目がない *Me ga nai*

"Have no eyes." (1) Be crazy about, like a lot. (2) Not know what one is doing.

(1) 彼はすしに目がない。

Kare wa sushi ni me ga nai.

He's got quite a weakness for sushi.

(1) 日本人は外国製の高級品には目がないようだ。

Nihonjin wa gaikoku-sei no kōkyū-hin ni wa me ga nai yō da.

Japanese can't seem to get enough of foreign luxury goods.

(2) 君を採用しないなんて、あの会社の人事部は目がないね。

Kimi o saiyō shinai nante, ano kaisha no jinji-bu wa me ga nai ne.

Their personnel section must be totally blind (have its head up its ass) if they aren't going to hire you.

● 目が離せない *Me ga hanasenai*

"Can't take one's eyes off." Can't take one's eyes off.

最近の国際情勢には目が離せない。

Saikin no kokusai-jōsei ni wa me ga hanasenai.

You've really got to keep your eyes riveted on international developments these days.

ヨチヨチ歩きの赤ん坊だけに全く目が離せない。

Yochiyochi-aruki no akanbō dake ni mattaku me ga hanasenai.

He's just a toddler, so you can't take your eyes off him for even a moment.

● 目が回る *Me ga mawaru*

"One's eyes go around." (1) Feel dizzy. (2) Be extremely busy.

(1) おなかが空き過ぎて目が回りそうだ。
Onaka ga sukisugite me ga mawarisō da.
I'm so hungry I feel giddy (it feels like the room is going around).

(2) 歳末は目が回るほど忙しくなりそう。
Saimatsu wa me ga mawaru hodo isogashiku narisō.
It's really going to be hectic around the end of the year. / I bet my head is going to be spinning (I'm going to be up to my neck in things to do) around year-end.

● 目に余る *Me ni amaru*

"Be too much for one's eyes." Be too much (a bit much), intolerable.

あの男の横暴ぶりには目に余るものがある。
Ano otoko no ōbō-buri ni wa me ni amaru mono ga aru.
I've had just about enough of him acting so high and mighty. / There's something about his highhandedness that is really too much.

あの政治家の企業への癒着ぶりには目に余るものがある。
Ano seiji-ka no kigyō e no yuchaku-buri ni wa me ni amaru mono ga aru.
That politician is much too cozy with business interests for me.

● 目に浮かぶ *Me ni ukabu*

"Float into one's eyes." Can picture, visualize.

彼女の慌てぶりが目に浮かぶ。
Kanojo no awate-buri ga me ni ukabu.
I can just imagine how excited she's going to be.

その情景が目に浮かんだ。
Sono jōkei ga me ni ukanda.
I could see the whole thing.

● 目にする *Me ni suru*

"Make something into an eye." See.

毛皮のコートを着ている人をよく目にするようになった。
Kegawa no kōto o kite iru hito o yoku me ni suru yō ni natta.

You run across more people wearing fur coats now than before.

「売り家あり」という張り紙を目にした。
"Uri-ya ari" to iu harigami o me ni shita.
I caught sight of a "house for sale" sign.

● 目につく *Me ni tsuku*

"Stick on one's eye." Stick out, catch one's attention.

派手なポスターが街のあちこちで目についた。
Hade na posutā ga machi no achikochi de me ni tsuita.
Colorful posters here and there throughout the city caught my eye.

背の高い彼女はどこへ行っても目につく。
Se no takai kanojo wa doko e itte mo me ni tsuku.
She is so tall that she stands out wherever she goes.

● 目に留まる *Me ni tomaru*

"Stop in one's eye." Get the attention of.

彼女の演技がプロデューサーの目に留まった。
Kanojo no engi ga purodyūsā no me ni tomatta.
Her performance caught the attention of the producer.

花屋の店先で、ばらの鉢植えが目に留まった。
Hana-ya no misesaki de, bara no hachiue ga me ni tomatta.
Some potted roses in front of the flower shop caught my eye.

● 目に見えて *Me ni miete*

"Can see it with one's eyes." Clearly, obviously.

病人は目に見えて回復していった。
Byōnin wa me ni miete kaifuku shite itta.
The patient was improving right before our very eyes. / The patient's condition had clearly improved.

彼の権力は目に見えて衰えていった。
Kare no kenryoku wa me ni miete otoroete itta.
It was obvious to everyone that his power was waning.

彼らのたくらみが失敗するのは目に見えていた。
Karera no takurami ga shippai suru no wa me ni miete ita.
Everyone could see that their scheme was doomed to fail from the very beginning. / It was a foregone conclusion that their plot would end in failure.

● 目の敵にする *Me no kataki ni suru*

"Make someone an enemy of one's eyes." Don't like someone's looks, hate someone's guts.

どうも彼は外国人を目の敵にしているようだ。
Dō mo kare wa gaikoku-jin o me no kataki ni shite iru yō da.
You get the feeling that he hates the very sight of a foreigner.

なぜ共産主義者を目の敵にするのですか。
Naze kyōsan-shugisha o me no kataki ni suru no desu ka.
Why have you got it in for Communists?

● 目を覚ます *Me o samasu*

"Wake up one's eyes." (1) Wake up. (2) Know better, wake up.

(1) 今朝、いつもより早く目を覚ました。
Kesa, itsu mo yori hayaku me o samashita.
I woke up earlier than usual this morning.

(2) いつまでバカなことをやっているんだ、いい加減に目を覚ませ！
Itsu made baka na koto o yatte irun da, ii kagen ni me o samase!
When are you ever going to learn? Get your act together!

See also 目が覚める *me ga sameru*.

● 目をつける *Me o tsukeru*

"Put one's eyes on something." Keep one's eye on, be interested in.

彼は警察から目をつけられている。
Kara wa keisatsu kara me o tsukerarete iru.
He's being watched by the police. / The police have zeroed in on him. / The police are onto him.

前からあの新型テレビに目をつけていたのだ。
Mae kara ano shingata-terebi ni me o tsukete ita no da.
I've had my eye on that new TV for a while.

● 目をつぶる *Me o tsuburu*

"Close one's eyes." Let something pass, wink at something.

今回のことは目をつぶっておきましょう。
Konkai no koto wa me o tsubutte okimashō.
I'm going to let it go this time. / I'm going to look the other way this once.

● 目を通す *Me o tōsu*

"Pass one's eyes over." Look at, look over.

彼は毎朝新聞に目を通すことにしている。
Kare wa maiasa shinbun ni me o tōsu koto ni shite iru.
He's in the habit of skimming the newspaper every morning.

この原稿に目を通してください。
Kono genkō ni me o tōshite kudasai.
Take a look at (look over) this manuscript.

● 目を盗む *Me o nusumu*

"Steal someone's eyes." Avoid being seen by someone.

子供たちは家の人の目を盗んでお酒を飲んだ。
Kodomo-tachi wa ie no hito no me o nusunde osake o nonda.
The kids sneaked a drink behind their family's back.

親の目を盗んでコソコソ男と会うとは何事だ。
Oya no me o nusunde kosokoso otoko to au to wa nanigoto da.
What do you think you're doing, slipping out and hanging around with guys without your parents knowing?

● 目を離す *Me o hanasu*

"Take one's eyes off." Take one's eyes off.

ちょっと目を離したすきに、盗まれたのです。
Chotto me o hanashita suki ni, nusumareta no desu.
Someone stole it when I looked the other way. / I just let it out of my sight for a moment, and someone stole it.

あの子は目を離すと、何をするかわからない。
Ano ko wa me o hanasu to, nani o suru ka wakaranai.
Take your eyes off that kid for a minute and she's up to something.

● 目を光らす *Me o hikarasu*

"Make one's eyes shine." Keep an eye on (as in surveillance), watch over someone's shoulder.

ガードマンが警備の目を光らせていた。
Gādoman ga keibi no me o hikarasete ita.
The rent-a-cop kept his eyes peeled.

刑事は容疑者の動きに目を光らせた。

Keiji wa yōgi-sha no ugoki ni me o hikaraseta.
The detective kept a close eye on the suspect's movements.

● 目を細める　*Me o hosomeru*

"Narrow one's eyes." Beam, smile with one's eyes.

母親は娘の踊る姿に目を細めていた。
Haha-oya wa musume no odoru sugata ni me o hosomete ita.
She beamed with delight (was bursting at the seams with pride) as
she watched her daughter dance.

ベビーカーの中を、老婆は目を細めてのぞき込んだ。
Bebīkā no naka o, rōba wa me o hosomete nozokikonda.
The old woman's eyes lit up when she peeked into the baby car-
riage.

Also 目を細くする　*me o hosoku suru.*

● 目を丸くする　*Me o maruku suru*

"Make one's eyes round." Be round-eyed, be astounded, one's
eyes get big.

子供たちは目を丸くして子犬を見ていた。
Kodomo-tachi wa me o maruku shite ko-inu o mite ita.
The children watched the puppies with wide-eyed interest.

乱暴な娘の態度に母親は目を丸くした。
Ranbō na musume no taido ni haha-oya wa me o maruku shita.
She was flabbergasted at her daughter's violent behavior.

● 目を向ける　*Me o mukeru*

"Turn one's eyes toward." Look at, consider, look toward, turn
to.

細かいことばかりではなく、全体に目を向けたまえ。
Komakai koto bakari de wa naku, zentai ni me o muketamae.
Try not to get too caught up in the little things. Keep the big pic-
ture in mind.

経済援助をめぐって、第三世界はますます日本に目を向けるだ
ろう。
*Keizai-enjo o megutte, daisan-sekai wa masumasu Nihon ni me o
mukeru darō.*
In all likelihood, Third World countries will turn more and more
to Japan for economic assistance.

● 目をやる *Me o yaru*

"Give the eye." Look at.

庭の桜の花に目をやった。

Niwa no sakura no hana ni me o yatta.

I looked at the cherry blossoms in the garden.

音のした方に目をやると、鳥が水浴びをしているところだった。

Oto no shita hō ni me o yaru to, tori ga mizuabi o shite iru tokoro datta.

When I looked in the direction the sound had come from, I saw some birds taking a bath.

● お目にかかる *Ome ni kakaru*

"To be hung on the eyes." Meet.

一度ゆっくりお目にかかって、お話を伺いたいと思っています。

Ichido yukkuri ome ni kakatte, ohanashi o ukagaitai to omotte imasu.

I hope to have the opportunity to speak with you at length sometime soon.

はじめてお目にかかります。私が山本です。

Hajimete ome ni kakarimasu. Watashi ga Yamamoto desu.

I believe this is the first time I've had the pleasure. Yamamoto is my name.

● 白い眼で見る *Shiroi me de miru*

"Look at with white eyes." Look askance at, give someone a
   dirty look, look daggers at someone.

容疑者の家族は皆から白い眼で見られた。
Yōgi-sha no kazoku wa mina kara shiroi me de mirareta.
The suspect's family was getting dirty looks from everyone.

老人は、彼女が未婚の母だというだけで、白い眼で見た。
*Rōjin wa, kanojo ga mikon no haha da to iu dake de, shiroi me
   de mita.*
The old man looked down on (looked down his nose at) her just
   because she was an unwed mother.

● 目と鼻の先 *Me to hana no saki*

"Right in front of one's eyes and nose." Right down the street,
   right over there; [of approaching events] impending, immi-
   nent.

その店ならすぐそこ、目と鼻の先にありますよ。
Sono mise nara sugu soko, me to hana no saki ni arimasu yo.
Oh, that shop? It's just a stone's throw from here.

不況は目と鼻の先まで来ているようだ。
Fukyō wa me to hana no saki made kite iru yō da.
A recession appears to be at hand (right around the corner).

● 目の上の(たん)こぶ *Me no ue no (tan-)kobu*

"A knot above one's eye." Someone who stands in one's way.

彼にとっては、直属の上司が目の上のたんこぶだった。
*Kare ni totte wa, chokuzoku no jōshi ga me no ue no tan-kobu
   datta.*
His immediate superior was a real thorn in his side.

姉の存在が、彼女には目の上のこぶだった。
Ane no sonzai ga, kanojo ni wa me no ue no kobu datta.
Her elder sister stood in her way.

● 目の玉の黒いうち *Me no tama no kuroi uchi*

"While one's eyes are black." As long as one is alive and kicking; [in the negative] over my dead body.

俺の目の玉の黒いうちは、お前の好きにはさせん。

Ore no me no tama no kuroi uchi wa, omae no suki ni wa sasen.

You're never going to get things your way as long as I'm around to see to it (I've got anything to say about it).

私の目の玉の黒いうちは、この土地は絶対人手に渡さない。

Watashi no me no tama no kuroi uchi wa, kono tochi wa zettai hitode ni watasanai.

The only way anyone will ever get their hands on that property is over my dead body.

Also 目の黒いうち *me no kuroi uchi.*

● 目の毒 *Me no doku*

"Poison for the eyes." The last thing one needs (wants) to see.

ダイエット中の私に、おいしそうなケーキは目の毒だ。

Daietto-chū no watashi ni, oishisō na kēki wa me no doku da.

Being on a diet, mouthwatering cakes were the last thing I needed.

若い女性の水着姿は、中年男性には目の毒だ。

Wakai josei no mizugi-sugata wa, chūnen-dansei ni wa me no doku da.

It's tough for a middle-aged guy to have to look at all those young things in their swimsuits.

鼻 HANA
Nose

We've all heard of horses or candidates for political office and other dubious characters winning something by a nose. Well, you can say the same thing in Japanese, at least about the ponies. *Hana no sa de katsu*—"win by a nose"—will do the trick. Aside from that part of the face that Japanese lay a finger on in reference to themselves, when we think they should be pointing to their chest, *hana* refers also to the sense of smell, as in the first of the idioms below.

● 鼻が利く *Hana ga kiku*

"One's nose works." (1) Have a good sense of smell. (2) Have a nose for.

(1) 僕は鼻が利くので、遠くでタバコを吸っていても臭いでわかる。

Boku wa hana ga kiku no de, tōku de tabako o sutte ite mo nioi de wakaru.

I've got a good nose, so I can tell when someone's smoking even if they're quite far away.

(2) あいつは本当にもうけ話には鼻が利く男だ。

Aitsu wa hontō ni mōke-banashi ni wa hana ga kiku otoko da.

The guy can really sniff out a deal. / He's got a nose for making money.

● 鼻で笑う *Hana de warau*

"Laugh with one's nose." Snort derisively, mock.

あの男はまだ子供さ、と彼は鼻で笑った。

Ano otoko wa mada kodomo sa, to kare wa hana de waratta.

"That guy never grew up," he sniffed.

彼女は僕たちの計画を鼻で笑った。

Kanojo wa boku-tachi no keikaku o hana de waratta.

She dismissed our plan with a snort.

● 鼻にかける *Hana ni kakeru*

"Hang something on one's nose." Be proud of, boast about, go on and on about.

彼は名門の出だということを鼻にかけていた。

Kare wa meimon no de da to iu koto o hana ni kakete ita.

He was bragging about graduating from a famous college.

彼女は、息子を有名な幼稚園に通わせていることを鼻にかけていた。

Kanojo wa, musuko o yūmei na yōchi-en ni kayowasete iru koto o hana ni kakete ita.

She prided herself on sending her son to some famous kindergarten.

● 鼻に付く *Hana ni tsuku*

"Hit one's nose." Be up to here with something, be sick (and tired) of something, have had about all of something that one can stand.

彼女には彼のいばった態度が鼻についた。

Kanojo ni wa kare no ibatta taido ga hana ni tsuita.

She was pretty fed up with his hoity-toity attitude.

あのレストランは味は良いのだが、ボーイ達の気取った態度が どうも鼻につく。

Ano resutoran wa aji wa yoi no da ga, bōi-tachi no kidotta taido ga dō mo hana ni tsuku.

The food at the restaurant is OK, but I haven't got much use for the waiters' pretentious attitude.

● 鼻の下が長い *Hana no shita ga nagai*

"The space below one's nose is long." Be soft on women, like the ladies, be a lady-killer.

「叔父さんは鼻の下が長い」と叔母さんが怒ってましたよ。

"Oji-san wa hana no shita ga nagai" to oba-san ga okotte mashita yo.

My aunt is really pissed about the way my uncle is always sniffing around the girls.

隣の酒屋のおやじは若い女の子が来ると、鼻の下を長くして喜 ぶ。

Tonari no saka-ya no oyaji wa wakai onna no ko ga kuru to, hana no shita o nagaku shite yorokobu.

The guy who runs the liquor store next door gets that twinkle in his eye every time a young gal comes in the door.

● 鼻を高くする *Hana o takaku suru*

"Put one's nose up." Be proud as a peacock.

高校野球で優勝したので、校長はすっかり鼻を高くした。

Kōkō-yakyū de yūshō shita no de, kōchō wa sukkari hana o takaku shita.

The principal is so proud that the team won the high-school baseball tournament you'd think he was going to pop all the buttons on his shirt.

売り上げが1位となり、支店長は鼻を高くしている。

Uriage ga ichi-i to nari, shiten-chō wa hana o takaku shite iru.

The manager is all puffed up since his branch came out number one in sales.

Also 鼻が高い *hana ga takai.*

● 鼻っ柱が強い *Hanappashi(ra) ga tsuyoi*

"The pillar of one's nose is strong." Stand one's ground, be defiant, ornery, feisty.

彼は彼女の鼻っ柱の強いところが気に入っていた。
Kare wa kanojo no hanappashira no tsuyoi tokoro ga ki ni itte ita.
He liked the way she wouldn't take any guff (shit) off anyone.

彼女は鼻っばしが強いけど、意外にやさしいところもある。
Kanojo wa hanappashi ga tsuyoi kedo, igai ni yasashii tokoro mo aru.
She's a feisty gal, but she can be surprisingly sweet, too.

Also 鼻っ張りが強い *hanappari ga tsuyoi.*

# 唇 KUCHIBIRU
Lip(s)

There are no famous sensuous Japanese lips; no Marilyn Monroe and no Andy Warhol to immortalize her. From a culture only now warming to the lure of the public embrace, it is too much to ask that lips play a prominent role in love lore. This may account, if nothing else does, for the sparsity of idioms focusing on the lips.

By the way, Japanese chickens don't have them either.

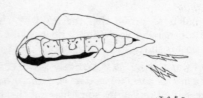

● 唇をかむ *Kuchibiru o kamu*

"Bite one's lip." Bite one's lip, be disappointed, be long-faced.

さよならホームランを打たれたピッチャーは、くやしそうに唇
をかんだ。

*Sayonara hōmuran o utareta pitchā wa, kuyashisō ni kuchibiru o
 kanda.*

The pitcher bit his lip in disappointment after he gave up a game-
winning homer.

個人投資家たちは株の大きな値下がりに思わず唇をかんだ。

*Kojin tōshika-tachi wa kabu no ōki na ne-sagari ni omowazu
 kuchibiru o kanda.*

The big drop in stock prices wiped the smiles right off the faces of
many individual investors.

● 唇をとがらす *Kuchibiru o togarasu*

"Sharpen one's lips." Complain, grumble; pout.

「家事ばっかり」と家内は時々唇をとがらしているよ。

*"Kaji bakkari" to kanai wa tokidoki kuchibiru o togarashite iru
 yo.*

The wife moans and groans that all she ever does is housework.

彼女は少しでも気に入らないことがあると、唇をとがらして文
句を言う。

*Kanojo wa sukoshi de mo ki ni iranai koto ga aru to, kuchibiru o
 togarashite monku o iu.*

She bitches about every little thing that doesn't suit her just right.

「お母さんは、妹ばかりかわいがる」とその男の子は唇をとが
らした。

*"Okāsan wa, imōto bakari kawaigaru" to sono otoko no ko wa
 kuchibiru o togarashita.*

"You always pay more attention to Sis than me," the boy
pouted.

You might run across the next expression in some romantic
potboiler, but people in the real world don't use it all that
much. I mean, after all, how many of us have ever actually
done it—or had it done to us?

● 唇を奪う *Kuchibiru o ubau*

"Steal someone's lips." Steal a kiss.

男は女の唇は奪ったが、心までは奪えなかった。
*Otoko wa onna no kuchibiru wa ubatta ga, kokoro made wa
ubaenakatta.*
The man may have stolen a kiss from her, but winning her heart
was another matter.

突然唇を奪われて、彼女はとても驚いた。
Totsuzen kuchibiru o ubawarete, kanojo wa totemo odoroita.
She was just floored when he kissed her all of a sudden.

口 KUCHI
Mouth

Kuchi has multiple meanings and appears as a suffix of
sorts in numerous compounds as well. In addition to that
part of the body into which we put food and various
poisons, *kuchi* also means what we "say" and figures in
many expressions related to both how, and how often, we
say what we say. *Kuchikazu no sukunai otoko*, for example, is a man of few words, a sort of Gary Cooper type.
Kuchi also means an opening resembling a mouth, such as
the mouth of a jar as in *kuchi no hiroi bin*—a wide-mouth
jar. It can mean a person when spoken of as a mouth
to feed, a bite of food or a taste, and finally, a share
of something or a "piece of the action," all of which
are *hito-kuchi*. It appears in compounds (with the *k*
sometimes changing to *g*) such as *tōzan-guchi*, literally a
mountain-climbing mouth, or trailhead, and often indicates the place where something begins, ends, or passes
through. In a related sense, it appears in a compound in-
dicating a job opening or *shūshoku-guchi*. But this is only
the beginning—the *jo no kuchi*, which, literally, is the
lowest division of sumo wrestling.

● 口がうまい *Kuchi ga umai*

"One's mouth is good." Be a slick talker, a smooth operator,
honey-tongued.

「口がうまいわね」と言いながらも、彼女は嬉しそうに笑った。
"Kuchi ga umai wa ne" to iinagara mo, kanojo wa ureshisō ni waratta.
She laughed happily and said, "You've got quite a line."

あの人は口がうますぎて、どうしても信用できない。
Ano hito wa kuchi ga umasugite, dō shite mo shin'yō dekinai.
He's just too smooth a talker to trust. / No way I'm going to trust him, the way he has with words.

● 口が軽い *Kuchi ga karui*

"Have a light mouth." Have loose lips, can't keep one's mouth shut, can't keep a secret.

高橋さんは口が軽いので気をつけた方がいいよ。
Takahashi-san wa kuchi ga karui no de ki o tsuketa hō ga ii yo.
Takahashi can't keep anything to himself (Takahashi's got a big mouth), so you'd better be careful what you say (around him).

あの人に秘密を話したのが失敗だね。口が軽いので有名なんだから。
Ano hito ni himitsu o hanashita no ga shippai da ne. Kuchi ga karui no de yūmei nan da kara.
Telling the secret to him was a big mistake. The guy's a notorious blabbermouth.

● 口が堅い *Kuchi ga katai*

"Have a hard mouth." Be tight-lipped, closed-mouthed.

彼はとても口が堅い。
Kare wa totemo kuchi ga katai.
He knows how to keep a secret (keep his mouth shut).

口が堅い君だからこそ、こんな話をしたのだ。
Kuchi ga katai kimi da kara koso, konna hanashi o shita no da.
I told you about it because I know you can keep your mouth shut.

● 口が過ぎる *Kuchi ga sugiru*

"Too much mouth." Say too much, go too far.

「少し口が過ぎるぞ」と彼は私をたしなめた。
"Sukoshi kuchi ga sugiru zo" to kare wa watashi o tashinameta.
"You're out of line, saying that," he scolded.

おせっかいだと言ったのは、私も口が過ぎたと反省している。
Osekkai da to itta no wa, watashi mo kuchi ga sugita to hansei shite iru.
I think I went a little overboard myself when I said it was none of your business.

● 口が滑る／口を滑らせる *Kuchi ga suberu / kuchi o suberaseru*

"Let one's mouth slip." Blab something, let something slip.

つい口が滑って秘密を話してしまった。
Tsui kuchi ga subette himitsu o hanashite shimatta.
I blurted out the secret before I could stop myself.

相手が口を滑らせて言ったことを、彼は聞き逃さなかった。
Aite ga kuchi o suberasete itta koto o, kare wa kikinogasana-katta.
He didn't miss a thing that the guy let slip out.

● 口が減らない *Kuchi ga heranai*

"Mouth doesn't decrease." Have diarrhea of the mouth, run off at the mouth, be a ratchet-mouth, a ratchet-jaw, long-winded.

全く口の減らない奴だ。
Mattaku kuchi no heranai yatsu da.
You're a real motormouth. / You just go on and on. / It's hard to get a word in edgewise with you. / Don't you ever shut up?

ああ言えばこう言うで、全く口の減らない子だ。
Ā ieba kō iu de, mattaku kuchi no heranai ko da.
You've got an answer for everything, don't you, smarty-pants.

● 口が悪い *Kuchi ga warui*

"Have a bad mouth." Be a badmouth, be critical of everything.

あいかわらず君は口が悪いね。
Aikawarazu kimi wa kuchi ga warui ne.
I see your tongue is as sharp as ever.

彼は口は悪いが、根はやさしい人だ。
Kare wa kuchi wa warui ga, ne wa yasashii hito da.
He's always trashing everything, but he's good at heart.

● 口から先に生まれる *Kuchi kara saki ni umareru*

"Be born mouth first." Be a born talker, a motormouth, a wind-bag, not know when to shut up.

子供の頃、口から先に生まれてきたのだろうとよく言われた。

Kodomo no koro, kuchi kara saki ni umarete kita no darō to yoku iwareta.

When I was little, people used to tell me that I must have been born with a big mouth.

あの人はおしゃべりで、口から先に生まれてきたような人だ。

Ano hito wa oshaberi de, kuchi kara saki ni umarete kita yō na hito da.

The guy talks so much you'd think he was born with the gift of gab.

● 口に合う *Kuchi ni au*

"Suit one's mouth." Suit one's taste.

このくらいの甘さが私の口には合っている。

Kono kurai no amasa ga watashi no kuchi ni wa atte iru.

This is about as sweet as I like things.

お口に合うかどうかわかりませんが、食べてみてください。

Okuchi ni au ka dō ka wakarimasen ga, tabete mite kudasai.

I don't know if you'll find this to your taste, but please try it.

● 口に気をつける *Kuchi ni ki o tsukeru*

"Be careful of one's mouth." Mind one's tongue, watch one's P's and Q's.

少しは口に気をつけたまえ。

Sukoshi wa kuchi ni ki o tsuketamae.

Watch your tongue.

私がうそつきだとは失礼な。口に気をつけろ。

Watashi ga usotsuki da to wa shitsurei na. Kuchi ni ki o tsukero.

That's pretty rude, calling me a liar like that. You'd better watch what you say.

● 口にする *Kuchi ni suru*

"Make something into a mouth." (1) Eat, feed one's face. (2) Say, express.

(1) 今日は、一日何も口にしていない。

Kyō wa, ichinichi nani mo kuchi ni shite inai.

I haven't had a thing to eat all day.

(2) 近ごろ、外交関係者はよく「管理貿易」という言葉を口にしますね。

Chikagoro, gaikō-kankeisha wa yoku ''kanri bōeki'' to iu kotoba o kuchi ni shimasu ne.

The latest buzzword in foreign-policy circles is ''managed trade.''

(3) お金のことは、あまり口にしない方がいいと思う。

Okane no koto wa, amari kuchi ni shinai hō ga ii to omou.

I think it would be better if you didn't bring up money too much.

● 口をきく *Kuchi o kiku*

''Work one's mouth.'' Talk, say; talk to, put in a good word for.

あの男とは二度と口をきくつもりはない。

Ano otoko to wa nido to kuchi o kiku tsumori wa nai.

I'm never going to talk to him again.

この会社に就職したいのなら、私が口をきいてあげましょう。

Kono kaisha ni shūshoku shitai no nara, watashi ga kuchi o kiite agemashō.

I'll put in a word for you if you think you'd like to work here (for this company).

TARO

● 口を出す／口が出る *Kuchi o dasu / kuchi ga deru*

"Put out one's mouth." Interfere.

あの人のことを見ていると、つい心配で口を出してしまう。

Ano hito no koto o mite iru to, tsui shinpai de kuchi o dashite shimau.

I can't help putting in my two cents out of sheer worry when I see him doing something.

お金は出すが口は出さない。

Okane wa dasu ga kuchi wa dasanai.

He'll put up the money (for the project), but he won't interfere (in the way it's run).

● 口を挟む *Kuchi o hasamu*

"Stick one's mouth in." Get one's two cents worth in, chip in, butt in, cut in.

私にも口を挟ませてもらえませんか。

Watashi ni mo kuchi o hasamasete moraemasen ka.

I'd like to say a word (put in my two cents) here if you don't mind.

私達の問題ですから、口を挟まないでください。

Watashi-tachi no mondai desu kara, kuchi o hasamanai de kudasai.

Since it's our problem, maybe you'd like to just stay out of it.

● 口がすっぱくなるほど *Kuchi ga suppaku naru hodo*

"Until one's mouth gets sour." How many times have I told you, tell over and over.

遅刻するな、と口がすっぱくなるほど言ったのに。

Chikoku suru na, to kuchi ga suppaku naru hodo itta no ni.

If I've told you once, I've told you a thousand times—don't be late.

口がすっぱくなるほど注意しても、あの子の言葉づかいはなおらない。

Kuchi ga suppaku naru hodo chūi shite mo, ano ko no kotoba-zukai wa naoranai.

I've told that child to watch his P's and Q's until I was blue in the face, but he hasn't changed one bit.

歯 HA
Tooth, Teeth

As a part of the mouth and therefore associated with speech, *ha* figures in many expressions concerning how things are said, whether deviously or straightforwardly. The most graphic of the idioms, though, is one that likens an empty space to a mouth missing some teeth, perhaps from the fact that an unfilled theater seat or vacant house is dark like the gap left by a missing tooth.

● 歯が浮く（ような）*Ha ga uku (yō na)*

"One's teeth are floating." (1) [About a grating sound] set one's teeth on edge. (2) [About someone's behavoir, especially flattery] nauseating, disgusting; make one want to gag.

(1) 私は黒板を爪でひっかいた時の、あの歯が浮くような音が大嫌いだ。

Watashi wa kokuban o tsume de hikkaita toki no, ano ha no uku yō na oto ga daikirai da.

Oh, the sound of someone scratching their fingernails on a blackboard really drives me up the wall (sets my teeth on edge).

(2) 歯の浮くようなお世辞はよしてください。

Ha no uku yō na oseji wa yoshite kudasai.

Don't you think you're laying (spreading) it on a little thick there? How about knocking it off. / I've just about had enough of your damn brown-nosing.

(2) 結婚式とはいえ、あれだけ歯の浮くようなスピーチもめずらしい。

Kekkon-shiki to wa ie, are dake ha no uku yō na supīchi mo mezurashii.

Even for a speech at a wedding, it's unusual to lay it on so thick.

● 歯が立たない *Ha ga tatanai*

"One's teeth don't stand up." Be too difficult for one, one is no match for something or someone.

あの男には全く歯が立たない。

Ano otoko ni wa mattaku ha ga tatanai.

I'm no match for him. / He's way out of my league. / I can't hold a candle to him.

郵 便 は が き

1 1 2 -

東京都文京区音羽
一丁目十七番十四号

講談社インターナショナル
愛読者カード係

お名前 NAME	
年　齢 AGE	☐ 女性　FEMALE ☐ 男性　MALE
ご住所・郵便番号 ADDRESS	
お仕事 OCCUPATION	国　籍 NATIONALITY

本書の内容、装幀などについてご意見をお聞かせ下さい。
Impression of this book (content, design, etc.)

Our aim is to promote cultural exchange between East and West.
We are interested in your suggestions. 今後の出版企画の参考にい
たしたく存じます。ご記入の上、ご投函下さいますようお願いいたします。

1. Title of book：＿＿＿＿＿＿＿＿＿＿＿＿＿＿＿
   書名

2. Where did you purchase this book？
   本書をどこでお求めになりましたか？

   ☐ at a bookstore　　　　　(name　　　　　　　　　　)
   　　書店にて　　　　　　　　　　書店名

   ☐ elsewhere　　　　　　　　(name　　　　　　　　　　)
   　　その他の場所で

   ☐ a gift
   　　プレゼント

3. How did you hear about this book？
   本書をどこでお知りになりましたか。

   ☐ at a bookstore　書店にて

   ☐ in an advertisement　広告で (name　　　　　　　　　)
   　　　　　　　　　　　　　　　　　新聞・雑誌名

   ☐ in a book review　書評・記事で (name　　　　　　　　)
   　　　　　　　　　　　　　　　　　　新聞・雑誌名

   ☐ other　その他　　　　　(　　　　　　　　　　　　　)

4. Suggestions for future books (author, subject matter, etc.)
   今後出版を希望される企画、作品、作家などをお聞かせ下さい。

こんなに難しい問題は、私にはとても歯が立たない。
Konna ni muzukashii mondai wa, watashi ni wa totemo ha ga tatanai.
A problem like this is way over my head.

● 歯が抜けたよう *Ha ga nuketa yō*

"Like missing teeth." Sparse.

客席は、歯が抜けたように空席ができていた。
Kyakuseki wa, ha ga nuketa yō ni kūseki ga dekite ita.
There were empty seats all around the hall. / The audience was conspicuous by its general absence.

街に移り住む人が増えて、その村では歯が抜けたように家々がなくなっていった。
Machi ni utsurisumu hito ga fuete, sono mura de wa ha ga nuketa yō ni ie-ie ga nakunatte itta.
With so many people moving into town, the village seems like a graveyard.

● 歯に衣を着せぬ *Ha ni kinu o kisenu*

"Don't wear any clothes on one's teeth." Be frank, outspoken, forthright; speak one's mind.

その評論家は歯に衣を着せぬことで有名だ。
Sono hyōron-ka wa ha ni kinu o kisenu koto de yūmei da.
That critic is famous for the way she gets right to the point (says exactly what she thinks).

彼は歯に衣を着せずにものを言う男だ。
Kare wa ha ni kinu o kisezu ni mono o iu otoko da.
He gets right to the point. / He doesn't beat around the bush (mince his words). / He speaks his mind.

● 歯切れがいい／歯切れが悪い *Hagire ga ii / hagire ga warui*

"Feel good (bad) when you bite down on something." [Positive] clear, articulate, terse, to the point; [negative] sloppy, evasive.

その話になると、彼女は急に歯切れが悪くなった。
Sono hanashi ni naru to, kanojo wa kyū ni hagire ga waruku natta.
She suddenly started beating around the bush when the subject came up.

委員長の歯切れのいい答弁は評判がよかった。
Iin-chō no hagire no ii tōben wa hyōban ga yokatta.
The chairperson's crisp reply was favorably received.

舌 SHITA
Tongue

As an organ essential to both digestion and speech, *shita* figures in numerous idioms about ingestion and articulation. It appears in interesting compounds such as *neko-jita*—a "cat's tongue"—to describe someone who cannot drink their coffee or eat their potatoes too hot, and *zessen*, which means a "tongue battle" or more naturally, a war of words. In this combination, *shita* is pronounced *zetsu*.

Tongues are standard equipment in Japan, but some politicians opt for the double model or *nimai-jita*. In other words, they come forked in Japan, too.

Bero is a more colloquial word for tongue, *berobero* an onomatopoeic word for licking.

● 舌が回る *Shita ga mawaru*

"One's tongue goes around (revolves)." Be able to talk (very well or fast), be a real talker.

あのアナウンサーはよく舌が回るね。
Ano anaunsā wa yoku shita ga mawaru ne.
That announcer can really rattle off the news.

女の子の方が、男の子よりも舌が回るようだ。
Onna no ko no hō ga, otoko no ko yori mo shita ga mawaru yō da.
It appears that little girls are a lot more talkative than little boys.

● 舌を出す *Shita o dasu*

"Stick out one's tongue." (1) Be playfully disturbed at something. (2) Thumb one's nose at someone.

(1) 彼は英単語の発音を何度も間違えて、舌を出した。
Kare wa Ei-tango no hatsuon o nando mo machigaete, shita o dashita.

He stuck his tongue out in frustration when he repeatedly mispro-
nounced the same English words.

(2) 彼は口では同情していたが、心の中では舌を出していたの
だろう。

*Kare wa kuchi de wa dōjō shite ita ga, kokoro no naka de wa
shita o dashite ita no darō.*

He may have said that he sympathized, but secretly he was probably thumbing his nose at you.

● 舌を巻く　*Shita o maku*

''Roll up one's tongue.'' Be taken aback, blown away, thun-
derstruck.

その投手の速球には、ホームラン王も舌を巻くほどだった。

*Sono tōshu no sokkyū ni wa, hōmuran-ō mo shita o maku hodo
datta.*

The pitcher had a fastball that even had the other team's big gun
rolling his eyes.

少女のピアノ演奏に会場の人々は皆舌を巻いた。

Shōjo no piano ensō ni kaijō no hitobito wa mina shita o maita.

The young girl played the piano so well that the audience was all
agog.

あご AGO
Jaw(s), Chin

It means the lower jaw, both upper and lower jaws, or the chin. When you hear *ago ga yowai* at ringside, you know that some boxer has a "weak" or "glass" jaw. Contrarily, about a guy who can really take a punch, you say *ago ga tsuyoi*.

Figurative meanings of *ago* include excessive talking or jawing and, less commonly, food or chow. Idioms exemplifying these meanings are included in the following selection.

● あごが落ちる *Ago ga ochiru*

"One's jaw falls." Mouthwatering, delicious, succulent, yummy, fit for a king.

この店のミートローフはあごが落ちるほどうまい。
Kono mise no mītorōfu wa ago ga ochiru hodo umai.
This place has got some meatloaf that'll get your juices flowing.

ああ、おいしい。あごが落ちそうなくらい。
Ā, oishii. Ago ga ochisō na kurai.
Ummm, this is fit for a king.

Also ほっぺたが落ちる *hoppeta ga ochiru.*

● あごが出る／あごを出す *Ago ga deru / ago o dasu*

"One's jaw is sticking out." Be bushed, worn out, done in, dog tired, dragging ass.

歩き過ぎで、あごが出た。
Arukisugi de, ago ga deta.
I'm beat (dead tired, burned out) from walking so far. / I'm all walked out.

こんな重労働が毎日続いたら、さすがの彼女もあごを出すだろう。
Konna jū-rōdō ga mainichi tsuzuitara, sasuga no kanojo mo ago o dasu darō.
If the workload keeps up like this much longer, even she's going to drop in her tracks.

The next expression is presumably from the unpopular habit among some Japanese of ordering people around by motioning with their chin and a slight flick of the head.

● あごで（人を）使う　*Ago de (hito o) tsukau*

"Use someone with one's jaw." Boss someone around, be bossy.

あの会社の社長は、あごで人を使うので嫌われている。
Ano kaisha no shachō wa, ago de hito o tsukau no de kirawarete iru.
A lot of people don't like the president of that company because he's such a slave driver.

彼は使用人をあごで使っていた。
Kare wa shiyō-nin o ago de tsukatte ita.
He was ordering his employees around.

首 KUBI
Neck

Kubi not only means "neck" as a part of the body, but like the English is also used to refer to the narrow part of a bottle. Since, unlike its literal English counterpart, *kubi* also means "head," *kubi o kiru* can mean either to cut someone's neck or to behead someone. Figuratively, it may also be used to mean one's life, since it is difficult to imagine life without a neck. Hence, if someone shouts at you *Kubi o yaru ze!*, it is best to take to your heels before he can get at your neck. Less threatening, but none the less unpleasant, is the threat *Omae wa kubi da!*, which you should recognize as a promise to have your head insofar as it means your job.

● 首が危ない　*Kubi ga abunai*

"One's neck is in danger." About to be get fired, on the verge of losing one's job.

このプロジェクトが失敗したら私の首は危ない。
Kono purojekuto ga shippai shitara watashi no kubi wa abunai.
If I lay an egg on this project, they're going to want my head.

首が危なくなるようなことは止めた方がいいよ。
Kubi ga abunaku naru yō na koto wa yameta hō ga ii yo.
You'd better not do anything that'll put your head on the chopping block.

● 首がつながる *Kubi ga tsunagaru*

"One's neck is connected." Manage to hang on to (keep) one's job.

彼のおかげで首がつながった。
Kare no okage de kubi ga tsunagatta.
Thanks to him, I managed to hold on to my job. / I didn't get fired because of him.

なんとか首がつながる方法はないだろうか。
Nan to ka kubi ga tsunagaru hōhō wa nai darō ka.
There must be something I can do to keep from getting fired.

● 首が飛ぶ *Kubi ga tobu*

"One's neck (head) flies." Get fired, get canned, get one's walking papers.

社長に知れたら首が飛ぶぞ。
Shachō ni shiretara kubi ga tobu zo.
If the boss finds out, heads are going to roll.

この事件が広まったら、僕の首はいっぺんに飛んでしまう。
Kono jiken ga hiromattara, boku no kubi wa ippen ni tonde shimau.
If this ever gets out, I'll be out on my ass real quick.

● 首が回らない *Kubi ga mawaranai*

"Be unable to turn one's neck." Be deep in debt, be in hock.

今月は借金が多くて首が回らない。
Kongetsu wa shakkin ga ōkute kubi ga mawaranai.
I'm up to my neck (ears) in debt this month. / I'm swimming in debt this month. / I'm really in the hole this month.

債務で首が回らなくなった企業が次々と倒産した。
Saimu de kubi ga mawaranaku natta kigyō ga tsugitsugi to tōsan shita.
Debt-ridden companies went belly up one after another.

● 首になる／首にする *Kubi ni naru / kubi ni suru*

"Become a neck." Get fired, get the ax (the boot).

僕は首になる前に自分から会社を辞めた。
Boku wa kubi ni naru mae ni jibun kara kaisha o yameta.
I quit before I got fired. / I quit before they could give me my
  walking papers.

「君を首にすることなど簡単だ」と部長がおどした。
*"Kimi o kubi ni suru koto nado kantan da" to buchō ga odo-
  shita.*
The manager threatened me by saying, "I can sack (can) you so
  fast it'll make your head spin."

● 首を切る *Kubi o kiru*

"Cut off someone's neck." Fire someone, let someone go, get rid
  of someone, lay someone off.

会社側が理由もなく君の首を切るとは考えられない。
*Kaisha-gawa ga riyū mo naku kimi no kubi o kiru to wa kan-
  gaerarenai.*
I can't imagine them sacking you for no reason.

いきなり150人もの従業員が首を切られた。
Ikinari hyakugojū-nin mo no jūgyō-in ga kubi o kirareta.
A hundred and fifty workers were suddenly out on the street.

● 首を突っ込む *Kubi o tsukkomu*

"Stick one's neck into something." (1) Get (jump, delve) into
  something. (2) Interfere, poke one's nose into.

(1) 彼はなんにでもすぐ首を突っ込む。
Kare wa nanni de mo sugu kubi o tsukkomu.
No matter what it is, he always jumps in with both feet.

(2) 君には関係のないことだ。首を突っ込んでくるな。
Kimi ni wa kankei no nai koto da. Kubi o tsukkonde kuru na.
It's none of your business, so just keep your nose out of it (just
  butt out).

● 首をひねる *Kubi o hineru*

"Twist one's neck." Wonder, have some doubts (reservations)
  about; ponder, think hard.

「本当かな」と彼は首をひねった。
"Hontō ka na" to kare wa kubi o hinetta.

"Really?" he wondered aloud.

出されたクイズに、回答者全員が首をひねった。
Dasareta kuizu ni, kaitō-sha zen'in ga kubi o hinetta.
All the panelists racked their brains trying to figure out the answer.

● 首を振る *Kubi o furu*

"Shake one's head." [横に *yoko ni*] shake one's head [as if to say "no"]; [縦に *tate ni*] nod one's head [as if to say "yes"].

信じられない、というように彼は首を振るばかりだった。
Shinjirarenai, to iu yō ni kare wa kubi o furu bakari datta.
He just shook his head in disbelief.

彼はようやく首を縦に振った。
Kare wa yōyaku kubi o tate ni futta.
He finally nodded his head (said OK). / He gave me thumbs up (the green light, the nod, the go-ahead) at last.

どんなに頼んでも、彼は首を横に振るだけだった。
Donna ni tanonde mo, kare wa kubi o yoko ni furu dake datta.
He just kept shaking his head (He wouldn't say yes) no matter what I said. / It was thumbs down no matter what I said.

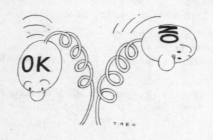

● 首ったけ *Kubittake*

"Up to one's neck (head)." Be infatuated with someone.

彼は彼女に首ったけだ。
Kare wa kanojo ni kubittake da.
He's head over heels in love with her. / He's nuts about (over)
her.

女性からのネクタイのプレゼントは、「私はあなたに首ったけ」
という意味なのだそうだ。
*Josei kara no nekutai no purezento wa, "Watashi wa anata ni
kubittake" to iu imi na no da sō da.*
When a girl gives you a necktie, it's supposed to mean that she's
crazy about (got a crush on) you.

のど NODO
Throat

There aren't many variations on the meaning of *nodo*.
Besides "throat," it can mean one's singing voice, hence
the *nodo jiman* or "proud throat" contests and programs
that choke Japanese television year in and year out.
Another more arcane meaning comes from the printing
world and refers to the white space between the facing
pages of an open book that collects dust and cookie
crumbs and is equally interestingly called a "gutter" in
English.

● のどが鳴る／のどを鳴らす *Nodo ga naru / nodo o
narasu*

"One's throat cries." One's mouth is watering, lick one's chops.

手作りケーキに、思わずのどが鳴った。
Tezukuri kēki ni, omowazu nodo ga natta.
My mouth started watering when I saw the homemade cake.

サラリーマンたちは仕事の後のビールにのどを鳴らした。
Sararīman-tachi wa shigoto no ato no bīru ni nodo o narashita.
The businessmen were smacking their lips as they gulped down
their beers after a hard day at the office.

● のどから手が出る *Nodo kara te ga deru*

"A hand comes out of one's throat." Really want, desperately need.

のどから手が出るほどあの車が欲しい。
Nodo kara te ga deru hodo ano kuruma ga hoshii.
I want that car so bad I can taste it. / I'm just dying to have that car. / I'd give anything to have that car.

いま彼がのどから手の出るほど欲しいものは、お金ではなく名前だろう。
Ima kare ga nodo kara te no deru hodo hoshii mono wa, okane de wa naku namae darō.
What he wants more than anything now is to be known, not to be rich.

背 SE
Back

In addition to that part of the human anatomy which we all love to have scratched, *se* also includes heights of things both animate and inanimate, as exemplified in the first few expressions that follow. If you ever go hiking in Japan, you'll soon become all too familiar with that part of a mountain range that this word refers to, the backbone or ridge, because few hiking trails in Japan follow the contours, favoring instead the grueling ridge route. Finally, *se* also means that part of a book that those of us interested in appearances often crack, even though we don't actually read the book. That's right, the spine.

● 背が高い *Se ga takai*

"Have a high back." Tall, high.

女性は、背が高い男性が好きですね。
Josei wa, se ga takai dansei ga suki desu ne.
Women like tall men.

最近背の高いビルがたくさん建ち始めた。
Saikin se no takai biru ga takusan tachihajimeta.
A lot of tall buildings are starting to go up.

● 背が低い *Se ga hikui*

"Have a low back." Short, squat, low.

私は父に似て背が低い。
Watashi wa chichi ni nite se ga hikui.
I'm short like my father.

背の低い家が道の両側に並んでいる。
Se no hikui ie ga michi no ryōgawa ni narande iru.
Low houses line both sides of the road.

● 背にする *Se ni suru*

"Make into a back." (1) Carry, shoulder. (2) Put (leave) something behind one. (3) Put one's back to something.

(1) 青年は大きなリュックを背にして山道を登って行った。
Seinen wa ōki na ryukku o se ni shite yamamichi o nobotte itta.
The boy climbed up the trail with a big backpack on.

(2) 村の人達の別れの言葉を背に（して）、彼は旅に出た。
Mura no hitotachi no wakare no kotoba o se ni (shite), kare wa tabi ni deta.
He started out on his journey, leaving the well-wishers from the village behind.

(3) 父は床の間を背にして座っていた。
Chichi wa tokonoma o se ni shite suwatte ita.
My father was sitting with his back to the tokonoma.

(3) 富士山を背に写真を撮りましょう。
Fuji-san o se ni shashin o torimashō.
Let's take a picture with Mt. Fuji in the background.

● 背に腹はかえられない *Se ni hara wa kaerarenai*

"One can't turn one's stomach into a back." Endure or do something because one doesn't have any other choice, there's no way around it.

背に腹はかえられない、と彼は条件の悪いその仕事を引き受けた。
Se ni hara wa kaerarenai, to kare wa jōken no warui sono shigoto o hikiuketa.
He had no choice but to take the job, even though the conditions weren't good. / It wasn't a very good job, but he figured he'd just have to tough it out and take it.

● 背を向ける *Se o mukeru*

"Turn one's back to or on." Turn one's back on something or someone, reject.

「さようなら」と言って彼女は彼に背を向けた。
"Sayōnara" to itte kanojo wa kare ni se o muketa.
"Goodbye," she said, and turned to walk away.

東欧諸国はマルクス主義に背を向けた。
Tōō-shokoku wa marukusu-shugi ni se o muketa.
The countries of Eastern Europe have turned their backs on Marxism.

肩 KATA
Shoulder

Aside from the bodily "shoulder," *kata* refers to that part of a shirt or jacket which goes by the same name in English, that section of the road where you pull off to change a flat or relieve yourself, and other shoulder-like protuberances such as the shoulder of a mountain.

Generally speaking, idioms with *kata* concern work or responsibility and the pressures resulting from them. There are several idioms, however, that express a person's attitude or bearing.

By the way, when a Japanese sports announcer says the right fielder has a strong shoulder, *kata ga tsuyoi*, he means, of course, that he has a strong arm.

● 肩が凝る *Kata ga koru*

"Have frozen shoulders." (1) Have a stiff neck. (2) Feel ill at ease, get (be) uptight.

(1) 肩が凝ったので、マッサージをしてもらった。
Kata ga kotta no de, massāji o shite moratta.
My neck was stiff so I got a massage.

(2) 社長がいると肩が凝る。
Shachō ga iru to kata ga koru.
I feel ill at ease whenever the boss is around.

(2) 肩の凝らない本を読みたいな。
Kata no koranai hon o yomitai na.
I'd like to do a little light reading.

● 肩にかかる *Kata ni kakaru*

"Be on one's shoulders." Be one's responsibility.

団長という責任が彼の肩にかかっていた。
Danchō to iu sekinin ga kare no kata ni kakatte ita.
The responsibilities of being group leader were squarely on his shoulders.

この国の将来は君たちの肩にかかっている。
Kono kuni no shōrai wa kimi-tachi no kata ni kakatte iru.
The future of the nation is in your hands.

● 肩の力を抜く *Kata no chikara o nuku*

"Remove the strength from one's shoulders." Relax, shake it out.

もっと肩の力を抜いて、気楽にやりなさい。
Motto kata no chikara o nuite, kiraku ni yarinasai.
Don't be so uptight. Take it easy and try it.

ふっと肩の力を抜いたら、いろいろなものが見えてきた。
Futto kata no chikara o nuitara, iroiro na mono ga miete kita.
As soon as I just relaxed a little, things began to fall into place.

● 肩を入れる／肩入れする *Kata o ireru / kata-ire suru*

"Put one's shoulder into something." Get behind something, be enthusiastic about something, support something, back something.

彼の学校は、昔からバスケット部に特に肩を入れている。
Kare no gakkō wa, mukashi kara basuketto-bu ni toku ni kata o irete iru.
His school has always been especially supportive of the basketball team.

その組合は、ある政党に肩入れしている。
Sono kumiai wa, aru seitō ni kata-ire shite iru.
The union is putting its weight behind a certain political party.

● 肩を並べる *Kata o naraberu*

"Line up shoulders." (1) Shoulder to shoulder. (2) Be on a par with, be neck and neck with, measure up to.

(1) 久しぶりに父と肩を並べて駅まで歩いた。

Hisashiburi ni chichi to kata o narabete eki made aruita.

For the first time in ages my father and I walked side by side to the train station.

(2) 彼と肩を並べる力士はいない。

Kare to kata o naraberu rikishi wa inai.

There is no other sumo wrestler that can even touch (come close to, hold a candle to) him. / He's head and shoulders above the rest of the wrestlers.

(2) 戦後、日本は経済大国として、先進国と肩を並べるようになった。

Sengo, Nihon wa keizai-taikoku toshite, senshin-koku to kata o naraberu yō ni natta.

Japan has grown to rival (joined the ranks of) the great economic powers of the world since the end of World War II.

● 肩を持つ *Kata o motsu*

"Hold someone's shoulder." Side (up) with someone, support someone.

田中さんの肩を持つわけではないが、彼に対する批判は間違っている。

Tanaka-san no kata o motsu wake de wa nai ga, kare ni taisuru hihan wa machigatte iru.

I don't mean to take sides with Mr. Tanaka, but the criticisms of him are not justified.

あなたはどうして彼女の肩ばかり持つのですか。

Anata wa dō shite kanojo no kata bakari motsu no desu ka.

Why are you always on her side? / Why are you always going to bat for her?

● 肩代わりをする *Katagawari o suru*

"Switch shoulders." Take over (for someone).

君の借金は、私が肩代わりしましょう。

Kimi no shakkin wa, watashi ga katagawari shimashō.

I'll pay off your loan for you.

● 肩たたき *Kata-tataki*

"Tapping someone on the shoulder." Early retirement.

私も、そろそろ肩たたきを覚悟する年になった。
Watashi mo, sorosoro kata-tataki o kakugo suru toshi ni natta.
I've reached the age where I'm likely to be put out to pasture
   pretty soon.

腕 UDE
Arm

In modern speech, *ude* refers to the whole arm, from the
shoulder to the wrist. Previously, it referred only to the
forearm, and *kaina*, a word no longer in general use, indicated the arm. Common compounds with *ude* include
udedokei or wristwatch, *udezumo* or arm wrestling, and
udemae or skill.

A guy's right-hand man is his *migi-ude*, or "right arm,"
but forget trying to figure out a catchy word for main
squeeze. *Aibō*, an old word still in use by men today,
originally referred to the guy on "the other end of the
pole" supporting a palanquin. This is about as close as
you can get in Japanese.

The idioms below are almost exclusively about skill—
getting it, proving it, improving it, and showing it off.

● 腕が上がる／腕を上げる *Ude ga agaru / ude o ageru*

"One's arm rises." Get better, improve.

君は、将棋の腕が上がったね。
Kimi wa, shōgi no ude ga agatta ne.
Your shōgi game is coming around (along).

ゴルフの腕を上げたければ、毎日の練習は欠かせない。
Gorufu no ude o agetakereba, mainichi no renshū wa kakasenai.
If you want to see some improvement in your golf game, daily
   practice is the ticket.

● 腕がいい *Ude ga ii*

"One's arm is good." Be skilled, good at, quite a hand at.

この店の板前さんは腕がいい。
Kono mise no itamae-san wa ude ga ii.
The chef here really knows his stuff. / They've got a great chef
here.

腕のいい仕立て屋さんを知りませんか。
Ude no ii shitateya-san o shirimasen ka.
I was wondering if you happened to know a good tailor?

● 腕に覚えがある *Ude ni oboe ga aru*

"One's arm remembers." Be good at something, be able to hold
one's own at.

私はスキーならば、少しは腕に覚えがある。
Watashi wa sukī naraba, sukoshi wa ude ni oboe ga aru.
I can handle myself all right on the slopes. / I know a little
something about skiing.

この老人ホームには、将棋なら腕に覚えがあるというお年寄り
が多い。
*Kono rōjin-hōmu ni wa, shōgi nara ude ni oboe ga aru to iu
otoshiyori ga ōi.*
Quite a few of the old folks here in this rest home say they are
pretty good shōgi players.

Don't be tempted to experiment too much with the following expression. It is used almost exclusively about cook-
ing.

● 腕を振るう *Ude o furuu*

"Shake one's arm." Show one's skill, go to town doing
something.

パーティーのために、腕を振るって料理を作った。
Pātī no tame ni, ude o furutte ryōri o tsukutta.
I cooked up a storm for the party.

彼女は隣の家族を夕食に誘い、自慢の腕を振るった。
*Kanojo wa tonari no kazoku o yūshoku ni sasoi, jiman no ude o
furutta.*
She invited the next-door neighbors over for dinner and laid out
quite a spread.

● 腕を磨く *Ude o migaku*

"Polish one's arm." Practice, brush up.

彼はゴルフの腕を磨くために、練習場に通っている。
Kare wa gorufu no ude o migaku tame ni, renshū-jō ni kayotte iru.
He goes to a driving range to improve his golf game.

お前の負けだ。腕を磨いて出直してこい。
Omae no make da. Ude o migaite denaoshite koi.
You lose. Come back and try again when you've done a little more practicing.

● 腕の見せどころ *Ude no mise-dokoro*

"The time to show one's arm." Time to show one's stuff, a chance to show what one can do.

彼は、ここが腕の見せどころ、とばかり張り切っていた。
Kare wa, koko ga ude no mise-dokoro, to bakari harikitte ita.
He was really up because he knew it was his big chance to strut his stuff.

お前の番だ。腕の見せどころだからがんばって来い。
Omae no ban da. Ude no mise-dokoro da kara ganbatte koi.
OK, it's your turn, kiddo. Get out there and show 'em what you've got (do your thing).

ひじ HIJI
Elbow

What you see is what you get, only one expression with *hi-ji*, namely *hijideppō* (elbow-gun). *Hiji*, aside from a few rare cases, just doesn't mean anything else. An elbow is an elbow—except on a chair, when it becomes an arm. An armchair is a *hiji-kake isu*, or literally, "chair with elbow rest."

You'll run into the behavioral counterpart of the first meaning of *hijideppō* on the crowded morning rush-hour trains in Japan. If you're really unlucky, you may get first-hand experience of the second.

● ひじ鉄砲を食らわす（食う）*Hijideppō o kurawasu (kuu)*

"Give someone an elbow-gun to eat." (1) Jab someone with one's elbow. (2) Rebuff someone.

(1) 彼女は、思いきり痴漢にひじ鉄砲を食らわした。
Kanojo wa, omoikiri chikan ni hijideppō o kurawashita.
She really let some pervert have it with her elbow.

(2) 彼は、彼女にひじ鉄砲を食わされて、しょんぼりしていた。
Kare wa, kanojo ni hijideppō o kuwasarete, shonbori shite ita.
He was moping around because she gave him the cold shoulder.

(2) 面接に行った会社からひじ鉄砲を食ってしまった。
Mensetsu ni itta kaisha kara hijideppō o kutte shimatta.
The company I tried to interview with wouldn't even give me the time of day.

胸 MUNE
Chest, Breast

Besides meaning chest or breast, *mune* can also mean one's mind or feelings, the lungs, the stomach, or the heart, either as an organ or as the seat of the emotions. In Japan, as in the West, the breast has long been considered the seat of the emotions. So it should come as no surprise that feelings of joy, excitement, and anticipation as well as those of sorrow and disappointment, which might be expressed in English by referring to the heart, are often conveyed in Japanese by idioms including *mune*.

When used in a compound, *mune* may be pronounced *muna*, as in *munayake* (or, also, *muneyake*) which literally means that one's heart is on fire, but actually that one has "heartburn." Similarly, to figure or count on something happening is expressed in the Japanese phrase *munazan'yō o suru*, which literally means to "count something in one's chest."

● 胸が痛む／胸を痛める *Mune ga itamu / mune o itameru*

"One's chest hurts." Painful, pitiful, heart-rending, heartbreaking, gut-wretching.

母の病気がとても重いことを知って、私の胸は痛んだ。
Haha no byōki ga totemo omoi koto o shitte, watashi no mune wa itanda.
My heart sank when I found out how sick my mother really was.

自分の不注意で花を枯らしてしまい、彼女は胸を痛めた。
Jibun no fu-chūi de hana o karashite shimai, kanojo wa mune o itameta.
She was heartsick because it was due to her own carelessness that the flowers died.

● 胸がいっぱいになる *Mune ga ippai ni naru*

"One's chest becomes full." Get a lump in one's throat, one's heart is filled with something [like joy], have one's heart in one's mouth.

故郷の写真を見ていたら、なつかしさで胸がいっぱいになった。
Kokyō no shashin o mite itara, natsukashisa de mune ga ippai ni natta.
I got all choked up with nostalgia when I looked at the pictures of my hometown.

思いがけない誕生日プレゼントに、彼女はうれしさで胸がいっぱいになった。

Omoigakenai tanjōbi-purezento ni, kanojo wa ureshisa de mune ga ippai ni natta.

Her heart was filled with happiness when she was given an unexpected birthday present.

● 胸が騒ぐ／胸騒ぎがする *Mune ga sawagu / munasawagi ga suru*

"One's chest clamors." Be excited, be worried.

息子が事故にあったその日は、朝から胸が騒いでどうしようもなかった。

Musuko ga jiko ni atta sono hi wa, asa kara mune ga sawaide dō shiyō mo nakatta.

The day my son had his accident I woke up in the morning feeling very uneasy (with a feeling that something bad was going to happen).

夫の出張先でテロ事件が起きたことを知り、急に胸騒ぎがした。

Otto no shutchō-saki de tero-jiken ga okita koto o shiri, kyū ni munasawagi ga shita.

She was worried sick when she heard that a terrorist attack had occurred where her husband was posted overseas.

● 胸がすく *Mune ga suku*

"One's chest is emptied." Be a load off one's mind, get something off one's chest.

単刀直入な彼の発言に、胸がすく思いがした。

Tantō-chokunyū na kare no hatsugen ni, mune ga suku omoi ga shita.

It was a real relief when he just spoke his mind.

その映画には、胸のすくようなラストシーンが用意されていた。

Sono eiga ni wa, mune no suku yō na rasutoshīn ga yōi sarete ita.

The movie had a last scene that left you feeling like a million dollars. / The movie ended with a cathartic scene.

● 胸がつぶれる *Mune ga tsubureru*

"One's chest is crushed." (1) Be scared to death. (2) Be choked with sorrow, all choked up.

(1) ああ、びっくりした。胸がつぶれるかと思った。

Ā, bikkuri shita. Mune ga tsubureru ka to omotta.
Jesus, you nearly scared the pants off me.

(2) 突然会社をクビになった友人の気持ちを考えると、胸がつ
ぶれて何も言えなかった。
*Totsuzen kaisha o kubi ni natta yūjin no kimochi o kangaeru to,
mune ga tsuburete nani mo ienakatta.*
I felt so bad when I heard that a friend of mine had lost his job
that I couldn't think of anything to say.

● 胸が悪い *Mune ga warui*

"One's chest is bad." Be sick to one's stomach; sickening,
revolting, disgusting.

不潔な調理場を見たら、胸が悪くなった。
Fuketsu na chōriba o mitara, mune ga waruku natta.
When I noticed how filthy the restaurant's kitchen was, I thought
I was going to barf.

あの男の名前を聞いただけでも胸が悪くなる。
Ano otoko no namae o kiita dake de mo mune ga waruku naru.
Just hearing his name makes me want to puke.

● 胸に描く *Mune ni egaku*

"Picture in one's chest." Imagine, see in one's mind.

彼女は楽しい学園生活を胸に描いていた。
Kanojo wa tanoshii gakuen-seikatsu o mune ni egaite ita.
She pictured living a carefree life at school.

あなたは子供の頃、どのような将来を胸に描いていましたか。
Anata wa kodomo no koro, dono yō na shōrai o mune ni egaite imashita ka.
When you were a kid, what did you see yourself doing when you grew up?

● 胸に聞く *Mune ni kiku*

"Ask one's chest." Ask one's heart; follow one's heart, let one's conscience be one's guide.

なぜそんなことになったのか、よく自分の胸に聞いてみなさい。
Naze sonna koto ni natta no ka, yoku jibun no mune ni kiite minasai.
Ask yourself why things ended up the way they did.

何度自分の胸に聞いてみても、やってないものはやっていないのです。
Nando jibun no mune ni kiite mite mo, yatte nai mono wa yatte nai no desu.
I've done a lot of soul-searching, but I swear that I just didn't do anything wrong.

● 胸に応える *Mune ni kotaeru*

"Affect one's chest." Cut one to the quick, tug at one's heart-strings.

彼女の批判は、当たっているだけに、胸に応えた。
Kanojo no hihan wa, atatte iru dake ni, mune ni kotaeta.
Her criticisms of me really hit home.

娘から「酔っぱらいは嫌い」と言われて胸に応えた。
Musume kara "yopparai wa kirai" to iwarete mune ni kotaeta.
It really cut me to the quick when my daughter said, "I just hate drunks."

● 胸に迫る *Mune ni semaru*

"Press on one's chest." Be moving, be touching; leave a strong impression.

この自画像は、何か胸に迫るものがある。

Kono jiga-zō wa, nani ka mune ni semaru mono ga aru.

There's something about this self-portrait that I just can't get off my mind.

彼のジャングルでの体験談には胸に迫るものがある。

Kare no janguru de no taiken-dan ni wa mune ni semaru mono ga aru.

His stories about his experiences in the jungle are stirring.

● 胸を打つ／胸を打たれる *Mune o utsu / mune o utareru*

"Strike one's chest." Touch, move, impress.

彼女の小説は、うまくはないが人の胸を打つものがあった。

Kanojo no shōsetsu wa, umaku wa nai ga hito no mune o utsu mono ga atta.

Her novel isn't much to get excited about, but there is something about it that really grabs you.

彼の言葉に、聴衆は胸を打たれた。

Kare no kotoba ni, chōshū wa mune o utareta.

The audience was moved by what he said.

● 胸を貸す／胸を借りる *Mune o kasu / mune o kariru*

"Lend someone one's chest." Give someone a workout.

横綱が弟子たちに胸を貸して、稽古をつけていた。

Yokozuna ga deshi-tachi ni mune o kashite, keiko o tsukete ita.

The yokozuna gave the lower-ranking wrestlers in his stable a chance to try their skill against him.

今日の対戦相手は、とても君たちの歯のたつチームではないが、胸を借りるつもりでがんばりなさい。

Kyō no taisen-aite wa, totemo kimi-tachi no ha no tatsu chīmu de wa nai ga, mune o kariru tsumori de ganbarinasai.

The team you're up against today is a lot better than you are, but think of it as good experience and give it your best shot.

● 胸をなで下ろす *Mune o nadeorosu*

"Rub one's chest downward." Be a great relief, a load off one's mind; reassuring.

救急車のサイレンに胸騒ぎを覚えたが、家族全員無事だったの
で、ほっと胸をなで下ろした。

*Kyūkyū-sha no sairen ni munasawagi o oboeta ga, kazoku zen'in
buji datta no de, hotto mune o nadeoroshita.*

The ambulance siren sent a shudder through me, so it was a load
off my mind when I found my family safe.

彼は、検査の結果がんではなかったので、胸をなで下ろした。

*Kare wa, kensa no kekka gan de wa nakatta no de, mune o
nadeoroshita.*

He heaved a sigh of relief when the cancer tests came back
negative.

● 胸を張る *Mune o haru*

"Stretch one's chest." Brag, be proud of, throw out one's chest,
puff up one's chest.

我が社の製品には個性がある、と社長は胸を張った。

*Waga-sha no seihin ni wa kosei ga aru, to shachō wa mune o
hatta.*

The president of the company proudly told us that each of his
company's products were distinctive.

自分で正しいと思うなら、噂など気にせず胸を張っていなさ
い。

*Jibun de tadashii to omou nara, uwasa nado ki ni sezu mune o
hatte inasai.*

If you think you're right, then just stand tall and don't pay any
attention to rumors.

● 胸をふくらませる／胸がふくらむ *Mune o fukura-
maseru / mune ga fukuramu*

"Expand one's chest." Be full of hope, be upbeat.

来月からカナダでホームステイすることになり、彼は期待に胸
をふくらませている。

*Raigetsu kara Kanada de hōmusutei suru koto ni nari, kare wa
kitai ni mune o fukuramasete iru.*

He is high on going to Canada next month for a homestay.

新婚生活への希望に、彼女の胸はふくらんだ。

Shinkon-seikatsu no kibō ni, kanojo no mune wa fukuranda.

Her heart filled with hope as she began a new life as a married
woman.

心臓 SHINZŌ
Heart

The several figurative meanings of *shinzō* derive both from its function as the organ that sustains life and from notions of the heart as the seat of the emotions. Hence a strong *shinzō* emboldens, a weak one enervates. As with "heart," *shinzō* can also be used to mean the center or most important part of, say, a factory or organization. Note that the first two idioms also carry the literal physiological meanings expressed.

Shinzō should not be confused with *kokoro*, which has no anatomical referent. Both may be translated as "heart," but the latter is not an organ.

● 心臓が強い *Shinzō ga tsuyoi*

"Have a strong heart." Have nerve, chutzpa, brass balls, heart, be brazen, be gutsy.

デパートで値切るとは、彼も心臓が強いね。
Depāto de negiru to wa, kare mo shinzō ga tsuyoi ne.
The guy's got a lot of cheek, bargaining in a department store.

私は心臓が強いらしく、どんなに大勢の人の前でも、あがらずにスピーチができる。
Watashi wa shinzō ga tsuyoi rashiku, donna ni ōzei no hito no mae de mo, agarazu ni supīchi ga dekiru.
I must be pretty nervy, the way I can give a speech in front of a lot of people without getting nervous.

● 心臓が弱い *Shinzō ga yowai*

"Have a weak heart." Be timid, shy, bashful; be a pussy, a wimp.

僕は心臓が弱いから、あまり脅かさないでくれよ。
Boku wa shinzō ga yowai kara, amari odokasanai de kure yo.
Don't scare me like that. I can't take that kind of stuff.

彼は心臓が弱いので、仕事で小さなミスをする度に、首になるのではないかとビクビクしている。
Kare wa shinzō ga yowai no de, shigoto de chiisa na misu o suru

tabi ni, kubi ni naru no de wa nai ka to bikubiku shite iru.
He's such a weenie that every little mistake he makes at work has
   him fretting about getting fired.

● 心臓に毛が生えている Shinzō ni ke ga haete iru

"Have hair on one's heart." Be brazen, a wise-ass, a smart aleck,
   cocky.

彼ほど図々しくて心臓に毛が生えているような男は見たことが
ない。

*Kare hodo zūzūshikute shinzō ni ke ga haete iru yō na otoko wa
   mita koto ga nai.*

I've never seen anyone that's such a wise guy.

彼は心臓に毛が生えているから、何を言われても少しも応えな
い。

*Kare wa shinzō ni ke ga haete iru kara, nani o iwarete mo sukoshi
   mo kotaenai.*

He's such a smart aleck that nothing you say to him makes any
   difference.

腹 HARA
Stomach, Belly

English speakers make up their mind, native speakers of
Japanese make up their bellies. So when Japanese intend
to do something adventurous, something calling for a
great deal of resolve—such as leaving the family business
to their daughter to manage—they might say something
like *Keiei o musume ni makaseru hara da*, or "I intend
to leave the running of the company to my daughter."
Another colorful expression with *hara*, *Kochira no hara
wa itamanai*, might best be translated as "It's no skin off
my nose" or "It's not costing me a thing." Neither *onaka*,
a polite synonym for *hara*, or *i*, a more anatomical term,
figure in very many idioms.

● 腹が黒い／腹黒い *Hara ga kuroi / haraguroi*

"Have a black stomach." Be evil, be blackhearted, be scheming.

あの男は親切そうに見えるが、実は腹が黒い。
Ano otoko wa shinsetsu-sō ni mieru ga, jitsu wa hara ga kuroi.
That guy looks like he's nice, but he's really a bastard (scumbag).

年寄りをだますような腹黒いまねはするな。
Toshiyori o damasu yō na haraguroi mane wa suru na.
Don't be a louse, cheating old people like that.

● 腹が立つ／腹を立てる *Hara ga tatsu / hara o tateru*

"One's stomach stands." Get angry, get bent out of shape, get
hot under the collar.

今度ばかりは腹が立った。
Kondo bakari wa hara ga tatta.
I'm really mad (pissed) this time. / I've really got my Irish (my
back) up this time.

そんなささいなことで腹を立てるのはよしなさい。
Sonna sasai na koto de hara o tateru no wa yoshinasai.
Don't get so riled (worked) up over something so stupid.

● 腹が出る *Hara ga deru*

"One's stomach sticks out." Have a little potbelly, have a spare tire.

運動もしないで飲んでばかりいると腹が出るよ。
Undō mo shinai de nonde bakari iru to hara ga deru yo.
If you keep drinking like that and don't get any exercise, you're going to end up with a spare tire (a beer belly).

年のせいか、最近腹が出てきた。
Toshi no sei ka, saikin hara ga dete kita.
I must be getting old. I'm starting to get a potbelly.

● 腹（が）へる　*Hara (ga) heru*

"One's stomach decreases." Get hungry, be hungry.

ああ、腹へった。何か食べるものある？
Ā, hara hetta. Nani ka taberu mono aru?
I'm starving. Is there anything to eat around here?

腹がへっては戦が出来ぬ。
Hara ga hette wa ikusa ga dekinu.
An army marches on its stomach.

Also おなかがへる *onaka ga heru.*

● 腹を決める／腹が決まる　*Hara o kimeru / hara ga kimaru*

"Decide one's stomach." Make up one's mind, decide, resolve.

大学に行くか就職するか、そろそろ腹を決めなければならない。
Daigaku ni iku ka shūshoku suru ka, sorosoro hara o kime-nakereba naranai.
I've got to make up my mind pretty soon whether to go to college or to get a job.

よし、これで腹が決まった。どんなことがあってもこの計画は実現させるぞ。
Yoshi, kore de hara ga kimatta. Donna koto ga atte mo kono keikaku wa jitsugen saseru zo.
That does it. My mind is made up. I'm going through with the project now, no matter what.

● 腹を割って話す　*Hara o watte hanasu*

"Cut one's stomach and talk." Have a heart-to-heart talk.

今夜は腹を割って話そう。
Kon'ya wa hara o watte hanasō.
Let's talk things out tonight.

腹を割って話してみて本当によかった。
Hara o watte hanashite mite hontō ni yokatta.
I sure did the right thing by having a heart-to-heart with him about it.

● 自腹を切る *Jibara o kiru*

"Cut one's own stomach." Foot the bill, pay for something when one doesn't really have to.

得意先の接待に、彼は自腹を切った。
Tokuisaki no settai ni, kare wa jibara o kitta.
He dug deep to entertain some of his best clients.

そんな高いパソコンに自腹を切るとは、すごいね。
Sonna takai pasokon ni jibara o kiru to wa, sugoi ne.
So you paid for an expensive computer like that out of your own pocket. That's really something.

へそ HESO
Navel, Bellybutton

For all practical purposes, *heso* just means somebody's bellybutton. But a stretch of the imagination allows Japanese to use *heso* in reference to things that resemble bellybuttons in one way or another—pooched out or sunken—like the little dimple in a beanpaste bun. This is not, however, a particularly common usage. One interesting combination that is frequently heard is *heso-magari*, or a "bent navel," that is, a screwball, a crank, or someone who otherwise deliberately deviates from the norm.

● へそが茶を沸かす *Heso ga cha o wakasu*

"One's navel boils tea." Be a big laugh, be a million laughs.

あいつが今では中学校の先生だとは、へそが茶を沸かす。

Aitsu ga ima de wa chūgakkō no sensei da to wa, heso ga cha o wakasu.

Imagine him a junior high school teacher—that's priceless (a riot).

あの汚職議員のキャッチフレーズが「クリーン…」とは、へそが茶を沸かす。

Ano oshoku-giin no kyatchi-furēzu ga "kurīn …" to wa, heso ga cha o wakasu.

That sleazy politician's "clean so-and-so" slogan has got to be the joke of the century.

● へそを曲げる *Heso o mageru*

"Bend one's navel." Get cross, be in a bad mood, get pushed out of shape.

みんなに子供扱いされて、彼女はへそを曲げてしまった。

Minna ni kodomo-atsukai sarete, kanojo wa heso o magete shimatta.

She was all out of sorts because everyone was treating her like a child.

彼は気に入らないことがあるとすぐへそを曲げる。

Kare wa ki ni iranai koto ga aru to sugu heso o mageru.

He gets bent out of shape every time something isn't going the way he thinks it should.

肝 KIMO
Liver

One of the few internal organs that figures in a significant number of idioms, the liver, or *kimo* in Japanese, also carries both meanings of the English word "guts": the innards collectively and the qualities of strength, fortitude, and bravery. A word of caution, however, is in order. *Kimo* is not used to refer to that cut of meat that so many children have nightmares about. At a restaurant, a butcher shop, or even a *yakitori* shop the word is *rebā*, the *katakana* approximation of the English "liver."

● 肝（っ玉）が小さい *Kimo(ttama) ga chiisai*

"Have a small liver." Be yellow, yellow-bellied, chicken-livered, chicken-hearted, lily-livered, fainthearted, weak-kneed.

彼はボクサーのくせに、肝っ玉の小さいところがあった。
Kare wa bokusā no kuse ni, kimottama no chiisai tokoro ga atta.
For a boxer, there was something about the guy that made him seem like a candy ass.

あの子は肝が小さくて、大きな音がするだけでびくっとする。
Ano ko wa kimo ga chiisakute, ōki na oto ga suru dake de bikutto suru.
That kid's such a sissy (scaredy-cat) that he flinches every time there's even a loud noise.

● 肝に銘じる *Kimo ni meijiru*

"Impress on one's liver." Take something to heart.

資源には限りがあるということを、一人一人が肝に銘じるべきである。
Shigen ni wa kagiri ga aru to iu koto o, hitori-hitori ga kimo ni meijiru beki de aru.
We should all bear in mind that the earth's resources are limited.

二度と同じ過ちを犯さぬよう、肝に銘じておきなさい。
Nido to onaji ayamachi o okasanu yō, kimo ni meijite okinasai.
Take this lesson to heart so that you won't end up making the same mistake again.

Also 肝に銘ずる *kimo ni meizuru.*

There is an important distinction between the next two expressions, although the English may on occasion be similiar. *Kimo o tsubusu* is used to express surprise; *kimo o hiyasu*, to express fear or danger.

● 肝をつぶす *Kimo o tsubusu*

"Crush one's liver." Be frightened out of one's wits, be blown away.

怪物のお面をつけて飛び出してきた子供に、肝をつぶした。

Kaibutsu no omen o tsukete tobidashite kita kodomo ni, kimo o tsubushita.

Some kid wearing a monster mask jumped out and scared the wits out of me.

目の前でオートバイ事故が起きた時は、肝をつぶすかと思った。

Me no mae de ōtobai-jiko ga okita toki wa, kimo o tsubusu ka to omotta.

It really floored me when that motorcycle accident happened right in front of my eyes.

Also 肝がつぶれる *kimo ga tsubureru.*

● 肝を冷やす *Kimo o hiyasu*

"Have a cold liver." Be scared (half) to death, terrified, scared stiff, scared spitless, nearly shit one's pants.

高層ビルの最上階にいる時に地震が起きたので、本当に肝を冷やした。

Kōsō-biru no saijō-kai ni iru toki ni jishin ga okita no de, hontō ni kimo o hiyashita.

I was scared out of my wits when I was on the top floor of a skyscraper and an earthquake hit.

会社に金の使い込みがばれてしまったのかと、肝を冷やした。

Kaisha ni kane no tsukaikomi ga barete shimatta no ka to, kimo o hiyashita.

Let me tell you, I was scared shitless when I thought they'd discovered that I had been siphoning off the company's money.

Also 肝が冷える *kimo ga hieru.*

手 TE
Hand, Arm

Sure, we say "tongues of flame" in English, but just because they lick at the walls doesn't mean they can't be called hands. That's what they are in Japanese, "hands of flame," *hi no te*. Unlike *ude* which only means arm, *te* can mean either hand or arm. It can mean paw, too, for that matter. In fact, there's a neat expression about being so busy that you want to borrow a cat's paw: *neko no te mo karitai-gurai isogashii*.

Second only to *me* in the number of idioms in which it appears, *te* has many other meanings, including, for example, that thing you grab to lift a pot or pan, its *hand*le; a worker or "hand"; someone's handwriting or their "hand"; a move as in chess or negotiations, or a particular way of doing something.

● 手が空く *Te ga aku*

"One's hand becomes empty." Be free, caught up (with one's work), have a minute.

斎藤君、手が空いたら私の部屋に来てください。
Saitō-kun, te ga aitara watashi no heya ni kite kudasai.
Saito, come into my office when you've got a minute (you're not busy).

今はとても忙しいので、夕方手が空く頃また来てください。
Ima wa totemo isogashii no de, yūgata te ga aku koro mata kite kudasai.
I'm swamped right now, but I should be caught up this evening. Come around again then.

Also 手がすく *te ga suku*.

● 手がかかる *Te ga kakaru*

"Take (occupy) hands." Take time, be a hassle, be a big job.

有機栽培は手がかかるそうだ。
Yūki-saibai wa te ga kakaru sō da.
They say that organic farming is quite a lot of work.

失恋のひとつやふたつで生きるの死ぬのと大騒ぎして、全く手のかかる奴だ。

Shitsuren no hitotsu ya futatsu de ikiru no shinu no to ōsawagi shite, mattaku te no kakaru yatsu da.

The guy's a real hassle, man. Gets dumped once or twice and goes off the deep end thinking it's the end of the world.

● 手が足りない *Te ga tarinai*

"Not have enough hands." Not have enough help.

年末は特に手が足りなくて困っている。

Nenmatsu wa toku ni te ga tarinakute komatte iru.

We're especially shorthanded around the end of the year.

肉体労働を嫌がる人が増えて、どこの工事現場でも手が足りないそうだ。

Nikutai-rōdō o iyagaru hito ga fuete, doko no kōji-genba de mo te ga tarinai sō da.

With fewer and fewer people willing to do manual labor, construction sites everywhere are suffering from a shortage of workers.

● 手がつけられない *Te ga tsukerarenai*

"Can't put one's hand on something." Be out of control, running wild.

彼は夕べから荒れ狂って、全く手がつけられない。

Kare wa yūbe kara arekurutte, mattaku te ga tsukerarenai.

He went bananas last night and has been completely out of control ever since.

彼女は昔、手のつけられないあばずれだった。

Kanojo wa mukashi, te no tsukerarenai abazure datta.

She really used to be a wild bitch.

よくもこんな手がつけられないほど散らかっている部屋に住めるね。

Yoku mo konna te ga tsukerarenai hodo chirakatte iru heya ni sumeru ne.

How can you stand to live in a room like this? It looks like a tornado just went through.

● 手が出ない *Te ga denai*

"One's hand doesn't go out." (1) Be too expensive for one. (2) Be too difficult for one.

(1) あまりにも高くて手が出ない。
Amari ni mo takakute te ga denai.
It's way out of my range. / I could never afford that.

(2) 厄介な問題で私には手が出ない。
Yakkai na mondai de watashi ni wa te ga denai.
This is one tough puppy. I don't even know where to start.

● 手が届く *Te ga todoku*

"One's hand reaches." (1) [Usually in the negative] reach, realize. (2) Painstaking, meticulous. (3) Almost [a certain age].

(1) 都心の庭付き一軒家なんて、一生働いても手が届かない。
Toshin no niwa-tsuki ikkenya nante, isshō hataraite mo te ga todokanai.
There's no way in hell I will ever be able to afford a house with a yard in the middle of town.

(1) その主人公は、もう少しで願いに手が届くというところで死んだ。
Sono shujinkō wa, mō sukoshi de negai ni te ga todoku to iu tokoro de shinda.
The hero died just when his goal was within reach.

(2) 痒いところに手が届くようなもてなしをしてくれた。
Kayui tokoro ni te ga todoku yō na motenashi o shite kureta.
They saw to my every need. / The service there left nothing to be desired. / They catered to my every whim.

(3) 彼女のお父さんなら、60に手が届くか届かないかというところだろうか。
Kanojo no otōsan nara, rokujū ni te ga todoku ka todokanai ka to iu tokoro darō ka.
Her dad? He must be pushing sixty or so, I'd say.

● 手が早い *Te ga hayai*

"The hands are fast." (1) Be fast to put the make on a woman. (2) Be quick to fight.

(1) あの男は女に手が早い。
Ano otoko wa onna ni te ga hayai.
He's a fast worker. / That dude moves quick. / He's a lady's man.

(2) あの男は口よりも手の方が早い。
Ano otoko wa kuchi yori mo te no hō ga hayai.
That guy doesn't waste time talking; he goes right into action
  (comes out fighting). / He shoots first and asks questions later.

● 手に入れる *Te ni ireru*

"Get something in one's hand." Get hold of, land.

ずっと欲しかった人形をやっとの思いで手に入れた。
Zutto hoshikatta ningyō o yatto no omoi de te ni ireta.
I finally got the doll I had wanted for so long.

この壺は知人に頼んで手に入れたものです。
Kono tsubo wa chijin ni tanonde te ni ireta mono desu.
This pot is one that I had a friend of mine pick up for me.

● 手に負えない *Te ni oenai*

"The hands can't take on." Be out of one's control, have one's
  hands full with something.

事態は手に負えなくなった。
Jitai wa te ni oenaku natta.
The situation got out of hand.

今度の仕事は私一人では手に負えません。
Kondo no shigoto wa watashi hitori de wa te ni oemasen.
This is one job I can't handle alone.

- 手にする *Te ni suru*

"Make into a hand." Gain, get, acquire, win.

こんな高価な物を手にするのは初めてだ。
Konna kōka na mono o te ni suru no wa hajimete da.
This is the first time I've ever had anything this expensive.

彼女は努力の末今の幸せを手にした。
Kanojo wa doryoku no sue ima no shiawase o te ni shita.
She kept plugging away and finally found happiness.

現役の議員が勝利を手にすることはなかった。
Gen'eki no giin ga shōri o te ni suru koto wa nakatta.
The incumbent congressman couldn't pull the election off (came up a loser).

- 手につかない *Te ni tsukanai*

"Won't stick to one's hand." Can't get down to, can't concentrate on.

宝くじの当選発表が気になって、仕事が手につかない。
Takarakuji no tōsen-happyō ga ki ni natte, shigoto ga te ni tsukanai.
I just can't seem to get down to work because I'm thinking all the time about who's going to win the lottery.

テレビの音がうるさくて試験勉強が手につかない。
Terebi no oto ga urusakute shiken-benkyō ga te ni tsukanai.
The TV is so loud that it's keeping me from studying for the test.

- 手に取るよう *Te ni toru yō*

"As if one could almost take something in hand." Perfectly, clearly.

彼の考えていることが手に取るようにわかった。
Kare no kangaete iru koto ga te ni toru yō ni wakatta.
I could read his thoughts like a book. / I knew exactly what he was thinking.

窓の下を通る人の話し声が、手に取るように聞こえた。
Mado no shita o tōru hito no hanashi-goe ga, te ni toru yō ni kikoeta.
I could hear people talking as clear as a bell as they passed below the window.

● 手に乗る *Te ni noru*

"Ride someone's hand." [In the negative] not fall for, not bite.

どんなにおだてても、その手には乗らないよ。
Donna ni odatete mo, sono te ni wa noranai yo.
You can soft-soap me all you want, but there's no way I'm going to fall for it.

泣いても、今度はその手には乗らない。
Naite mo, kondo wa sono te ni wa noranai.
Cry all you want. I'm not buying it, not this time.

● 手に渡る *Te ni wataru*

"Cross into one's hand." Be passed on to.

権力はタカ派の手に渡った。
Kenryoku wa taka-ha no te ni watatta.
Power was passed on to the hawks.

宝物のありかを書いた地図が、盗賊の手に渡ってしまった。
Takaramono no arika o kaita chizu ga, tōzoku no te ni watatte shimatta.
The map showing the location of the hidden treasure fell into the hands of some robbers.

● 手の内を読む *Te no uchi o yomu*

"Read someone's palm." Read, see through.

相手チームにすっかり手の内を読まれてしまった。
Aite-chīmu ni sukkari te no uchi o yomarete shimatta.
The other team saw right through us. / The other team read our every move.

相手の手の内を先に読んだ方が勝ちだ。
Aite no te no uchi o saki ni yonda hō ga kachi da.
Whichever side is first to figure out what the other side is up to is going to win.

● 手も足も出ない *Te mo ashi mo denai*

"Neither hands nor feet will move out." Be unable to do something, can't handle, can't get to first base.

柔道3段の田中さんが相手では手も足も出ない。
Jūdō san-dan no Tanaka-san ga aite de wa te mo ashi mo denai.

I don't have a snowball's chance in hell up against a guy like
  Tanaka, who's got a third-degree black belt in Jūdō.

数学の試験問題は難しくて手も足も出なかった。
*Sūgaku no shiken-mondai wa muzukashikute te mo ashi mo
  denakatta.*
The problems on the math test were so difficult that I didn't even
  know where to start (knew I was in over my head).

● 手を打つ *Te o utsu*

"Hit one's hand." (1) Do something (about), make a move. (2)
  Shake (hands) on it.

(1) 冗談を言うほかには、手の打ちようがなかった。
Jōdan o iu hoka ni wa, te no uchiyō ga nakatta.
I'm afraid there wasn't much we could do except laugh it off.

(1) 今すぐ手を打たなければ、環境は破壊される。
Ima sugu te o utanakereba, kankyō wa hakai sareru.
If we don't do something right away, the environment will be
  destroyed.

(2) 仕方がない、500万円で手を打ちましょう。
Shikata ga nai, gohyaku-man-en de te o uchimashō.
Well, all right, five million yen it is. Let's shake on it.

● 手を変え品を変え *Te o kae shina o kae*

"Change hands and change products." Every possible means,
  every trick in the book, the whole bag of tricks.

彼は手を変え品を変え、彼女の機嫌を取ろうとしていた。
Kare wa te o kae shina o kae, kanojo no kigen o torō to shite ita.
He tried everything under the sun to get on her good side.

セールスマンは手を変え品を変え、商品を売りつけようとし
た。
Sērusuman wa te o kae shina o kae, shōhin o uritsukeyō to shita.
This salesman tried more ways than you could shake a stick at to
  get me to buy something.

Also あの手この手（を使う）*ano te kono te (o tsukau).*

● 手を貸す *Te o kasu*

"Lend a hand." Lend a hand.

ちょっと手を貸してもらえませんか。
Chotto te o kashite moraemasen ka.
Would you mind giving me a hand for a second?

山崎は、自分の兄弟を殺す謀略に手を貸した。
Yamazaki wa, jibun no kyōdai o korosu bōryaku ni te o kashita.
Yamazaki helped engineer a scheme to kill his own brother.

● 手を切る *Te o kiru*

"Cut one's hand." Be through with something, cut something loose.

「この仕事を最後に、あの連中とは手を切る」と彼は言った。
"Kono shigoto o saigo ni, ano renchū to wa te o kiru" to kare wa itta.
He said, "This is the last job I'm doing with those scumbags. I'm calling it quits."

See also 足を洗う *ashi o arau.*

● 手を染める *Te o someru*

"Dye one's hand." Start, begin, get involved.

彼は悪事に手を染めてしまった。
Kare wa akuji ni te o somete shimatta.
He went bad. / He got mixed up with the wrong people.

株に手を染めて大失敗した。
Kabu ni te o somete dai-shippai shita.
He tried his hand at the stock market and fell flat on his face.

● 手を出す *Te o dasu*

"Stick out one's hand." (1) Throw a punch. (2) Get involved in. (3) Put the make on.

(1) あのデブが先に手を出したんだ。
Ano debu ga saki ni te o dashitan da.
That fat mother threw the first punch (started it).

(2) 競馬に手を出すべきではなかった。
Keiba ni te o dasu beki de wa nakatta.
I should have never started playing the ponies.

(3) 俺の女に手を出すな。

Ore no onna ni te o dasu na.
Keep away from my woman. / You best not be trying to put a
move on my woman, Jack.

● 手を使う *Te o tsukau*

"Use a hand." Use some way, use some means.

彼は不正な手を使って、その土地をものにした。
Kare wa fusei na te o tsukatte, sono tochi o mono ni shita.
He got that land in an underhanded way.

どんな手を使っても、この計画は成功させる。
Donna te o tsukatte mo, kono keikaku wa seikō saseru.
I don't care how I do it, but I'm going to see that this project
makes it.

● 手を尽くす *Te o tsukusu*

"Use up all one's hands." Try everything, do one's best.

彼女の行方を八方手を尽くして捜した。
Kanojo no yukue o happō te o tsukushite sagashita.
I did my level best to find her.

医者は、出来るかぎりの手は尽くしたが、患者はやはり手遅れ
だった。
*Isha wa, dekiru kagiri no te wa tsukushita ga, kanja wa yahari te-
okure datta.*
The doctors did everything they could, but the patient was too
far gone.

● 手をつける *Te o tsukeru*

"Put one's hand on." (1) Start, begin. (2) Screw, lay (a woman).
(3) Embezzle money.

(1) そろそろ次の仕事に手をつけよう。
Sorosoro tsugi no shigoto ni te o tsukeyō.
I guess I'm about ready to get started on something else.

(1) 片づけたくても、散らかり過ぎて、どこから手をつけたら
いいのかわからない。
*Katazuketakute mo, chirakarisugite, doko kara te o tsuketara ii
no ka wakaranai.*
I'd really like to straighten up the place, but it's so cluttered I
don't know where to begin.

(2) あの教師は、生徒に手をつけて学校を首になった。

Ano kyōshi wa, seito ni te o tsukete gakkō o kubi ni natta.

That teacher got fired for poking (fooling around with) one of
  the students.

(3) 彼は、会社の金に手をつけてとうとう首になった。

Kare wa, kaisha no kane ni te o tsukete tōtō kubi ni natta.

He was caught with his hand in the till and ended up getting fired.

● 手を抜く *Te o nuku*

''Pull one's hand out.'' Cut corners, skate.

彼は最近仕事の手を抜いている。

Kare wa saikin shigoto no te o nuite iru.

Recently he's been skating on the job.

あの業者は工事の手を抜いて訴えられた。

Ano gyōsha wa kōji no te o nuite uttaerareta.

The contractor was sued for cutting corners on his buildings (for
  shoddy construction practices).

● 手を広げる *Te o hirogeru*

''Spread out one's hands.'' Expand, diversify.

彼はホテル経営にまで手を広げた。

Kare wa hoteru-keiei ni made te o hirogeta.

He expanded into the hotel business.

会社は手を広げすぎて倒産した。

Kaisha wa te o hirogesugite tōsan shita.

The company overextended itself and went under.

● 手を引く *Te o hiku*

''Pull one's hand.'' Leave, get out, back out, drop out, give
  something up.

政治情勢は不安定だが、アメリカの企業はそれだけでその国か
ら手を引くことはないだろう。

*Seiji-jōsei wa fu-antei da ga, Amerika no kigyō wa sore dake de
  sono kuni kara te o hiku koto wa nai darō.*

American businesses are not going to pull up stakes just because
  the political situation in the country is unstable.

私はこの計画から手を引かせてもらう。

Watashi wa kono keikaku kara te o hikasete morau.
I'm pulling out of this project.

● 手を焼く *Te o yaku*

"Burn one's hand." Have one's hands full.

あの子供には手を焼くよ。
Ano kodomo ni wa te o yaku yo.
That kid is a real handful.

メーカーは電気自動車の設計に手を焼いている。
Mēkā wa denki-jidōsha no sekkei ni te o yaite iru.
Automobile manufacturers are having trouble designing an electric car.

● 手を休める *Te o yasumeru*

"Give one's hand a rest." Take a break, stop doing something.

お姉さん、ちょっと手を休めてテレビゲームでもやろうよ。
Onē-san, chotto te o yasumete terebi-gēmu de mo yarō yo.
Come on, Sis, put down what you're doing and let's play a video game or something.

母は編み物の手を休めて、テレビを見た。
Haha wa amimono no te o yasumete, terebi o mita.
Mom put down her knitting to watch TV for a while.

指 YUBI
Finger

It should come as no surprise that all five fingers have Japanese names, starting with the thumb or *oya-yubi* (parent finger). Japanese women use their thumb to indicate a man by raising it in a "thumbs up" gesture, often accompanied by a comment like *Kore ga urusai*, which roughly means that their boyfriend or husband won't let them do what they want to do. The index finger is called the *hitosashi-yubi*, or the finger you use to point at people. Known only as the *naka-yubi* (middle finger), the longest finger on the hand comes out short in the name game. The ring finger is known as the *kusuri-yubi* or "medicine finger" because, being the weakest of the fingers and therefore the least likely to inflict pain, it's the one that was traditionally used to mix and apply concoctions of all kinds to injuries. The last and least is the *ko-yubi*, or "little finger," which gets a lot of use by Japanese men, who make a fist and stick it up when they're talking about women or their amorous adventures.

By the way, closing the index finger and the thumb in a circle, as an American might do to make the OK sign, means "money," though it can also be used for OK. If it's toes that you want to talk about, just affix *ashi no* to *yubi* and you have, quite logically, a "foot finger."

● 指一本（も）触れさせない　*Yubi ippon (mo) furesasenai*

"Not let someone lay even one finger on something." Don't let someone lay a finger on.

彼女には指一本触れさせない。
Kanojo ni wa yubi ippon furesasenai.
You lay even so much as one finger on her! / Lay a finger on her and you're in for it!

先祖代々のこの土地に、誰であろうと、指一本も触れさせない。
Senzo-daidai no kono tochi ni, dare de arō to, yubi ippon mo furesasenai.
This property has been in the family for generations, and I'm not about to let anyone lay a finger on it (get their hands on it).

● 指をくわえる　*Yubi o kuwaeru*

"Have one's finger in one's mouth." (1) Stand around (without doing anything). (2) Look on longingly.

(1) 彼が乱暴されているのを、指をくわえて見ていたというのか。
Kare ga ranbō sarete iru no o, yubi o kuwaete mite ita to iu no ka.
You mean you just stood there and watched while he was being assaulted? / Don't tell me you just stood around with your finger in your ear (picking your nose) while he was getting beaten up?

(2) 彼は幸せそうな家族の姿を、指をくわえて見ていた。

Kare wa shiawase-sō na kazoku no sugata o, yubi o kuwaete mite ita.

He watched the happy family enviously.

● 後ろ指をさされる *Ushiro-yubi o sasareru*

"Be pointed at behind one's back." Be the object of gossip.

私は、後ろ指をさされるようなことは何もしていない。

Watashi wa, ushiro-yubi o sasareru yō na koto wa nani mo shite inai.

I haven't done anything to make people talk behind my back.

人から後ろ指をさされるようなことだけは、してはならない。

Hito kara ushiro-yubi o sasareru yō na koto dake wa, shite wa naranai.

Don't do anything that will cause you to be the object of gossip.

爪 TSUME
Fingernail, Claw

This is one of those words that you can use for several similar things that require different words in English. People have fingernails, cats claws, and birds of prey talons, but in Japanese they all simply have *tsume*. Other meanings of the word include picks or plectrums, the prongs or claws that hold a gemstone in the setting of a ring, and other such devices that hold things in place. *Tsume* is also used to mean an extremely small amount of something.

Lighting your fingernail instead of a candle is certainly one way to cut back on expenses, I suppose. The first expression below evokes an interesting image that should make it easy to remember. In English, a person so inclined is nothing other than a skinflint!

● 爪に火をともす *Tsume ni hi o tomosu*

"Light one's fingernail." Be very frugal, tightfisted.

この100万円は、爪に火をともすようにして貯めたお金です。

Kono hyaku-man-en wa, tsume ni hi o tomosu yō ni shite tameta okane desu.

I pinched pennies to save up this million yen.

私が爪に火をともすようにして貯めたお金を、彼は博打で一晩のうちになくしてしまった。

Watashi ga tsume ni hi o tomosu yō ni shite tameta okane o, kare wa bakuchi de hitoban no uchi ni nakushite shimatta.

In one night at the tables he blew all the money I had scrimped and saved to get.

● 爪の垢をせんじて飲む *Tsume no aka o senjite nomu*

"Boil the dirt from someone's nails and drink it." Emulate someone, try to be like someone.

僕も頭がよくなるように、君の爪の垢をせんじて飲ませてくれ。

Boku mo atama ga yoku naru yō ni, kimi no tsume no aka o senjite nomasete kure.

I just want to be smart like you. Tell me what I should do.

田中さんの爪の垢をせんじて飲みなさい。
Tanaka-san no tsume no aka o senjite nominasai.
You ought to take a lesson from Tanaka.

● 爪を研ぐ *Tsume o togu*

"Sharpen one's claws." Wait for an opportunity to do something.

彼は、逆転ホームランを打つチャンスを、爪を研いで狙っていた。
Kare wa, gyakuten-hōmuran o utsu chansu o, tsume o toide neratte ita.
He was licking his chops at the chance to hit a homer that would turn the game around.

彼は長い間、復讐の爪を研いできた。
Kare wa nagai aida, fukushū no tsume o toide kita.
He waited a long time for a chance to get even.

腰 KOSHI
Waist, Hips

Koshi is defined in dictionaries as the part of the body where the legs are attached to the trunk, wherever that might be. Hips is perhaps the most common translation of the word, but waist is also frequently used. When Japanese talk about it hurting, *koshi ga itai*, then it's safe to say that they mean their lower back.

It is considered in many oriental cultures to be the part of the body from which power comes, so idioms including *koshi* often refer to physical strength and willpower or their absence.

Koshi also refers to a certain elusive quality of noodles, rice cakes, *mochi* and even paper. Basically, to have it is good and not to have it is bad. It might best be described as firmness or chewiness when those qualities are desirable in a food.

● 腰が重い *Koshi ga omoi*

"Be heavy-hipped." Be prone to stay somewhere a long time; have lead in one's pants, be nailed to the floor, be slow to act, sit on one's hands.

官庁は腰が重い、とよく批判される。

Kanchō wa koshi ga omoi, to yoku hihan sareru.

Government agencies are notorious for being as slow as molasses in winter.

彼はやっと重い腰を上げる気になった。

Kare wa yatto omoi koshi o ageru ki ni natta.

He finally got off his duff (made a move).

● 腰が高い *Koshi ga takai*

"Have a high waist." Be impolite, high-handed, arrogant, hoity-toity.

あの店の主人は腰が高いので客が少ない。

Ano mise no shujin wa koshi ga takai no de kyaku ga sukunai.

The guy who runs that store is so snooty that he doesn't have many customers.

彼は名門の出ということが自慢で、とても腰が高い。

Kare wa meimon no de to iu koto ga jiman de, totemo koshi ga takai.

He is so stuck-up just because he graduated from some famous school.

● 腰が強い *Koshi ga tsuyoi*

"Have strong hips." (1) Be determined, hang tough, unbending, resolute. (2) [Of food] chewy; [of paste or glue] sticky; [of a brush or paper] firm.

(1) 彼は腰が強いので、いつでも自分の思い通りにする。

Kare wa koshi ga tsuyoi no de, itsu de mo jibun no omoidōri ni suru.

He's the strong-willed type who always does things his own way.

(2) この餅は腰が強い。

Kono mochi wa koshi ga tsuyoi.

This mochi is nice and chewy.

● 腰が抜ける／腰を抜かす *Koshi ga nukeru / koshi o nukasu*

"One's hips drop out." Be so surprised that one is unable to move.

腰が抜けるほどびっくりした。
Koshi ga nukeru hodo bikkuri shita.
That surprised the heck out of me. / I was floored.

これから僕の話すことにびっくりして腰を抜かすなよ。
Kore kara boku no hanasu koto ni bikkuri shite koshi o nukasu na yo.
Now don't let what I'm going to say throw you for a loop.

● 腰が低い *Koshi ga hikui*

"Have a low waist." Be courteous, humble, polite, have a low profile.

あの店のおやじさんは本当に腰が低い。
Ano mise no oyaji-san wa hontō ni koshi ga hikui.
The old guy that works there is really courteous.

今日、とても腰の低いセールスマンが来た。
Kyō, totemo koshi no hikui sērusuman ga kita.
A very polite salesman came by today.

● 腰が弱い *Koshi ga yowai*

"Have weak hips." (1) Be weak-kneed, give up quickly. (2) [Of food] not be chewy; [of paste or glue] not be very sticky; [of a brush or paper] be limp, weak.

(1) あの男は腰が弱いので、交渉には向かないだろう。
Ano otoko wa koshi ga yowai no de, kōshō ni wa mukanai darō.
That guy's such a pushover that he wouldn't be much of a negotiator.

(2) この紙は腰が弱いのですぐ破ける。
Kono kami wa koshi ga yowai no de sugu yabukeru.
This paper tears easily because there's not much to it.

● 腰を入れる／本腰を入れる *Koshi o ireru / hongoshi o ireru*

"Put one's (main) hips into something." Throw oneself into something, put one's shoulder to the wheel.

息子がようやく商売に腰を入れ始めた。
Musuko ga yōyaku shōbai ni koshi o irehajimeta.

My son finally started to put his back into the business.

彼はコンクールに出品するために、本腰を入れて制作を始めた。

Kare wa konkūru ni shuppin suru tame ni, hongoshi o irete seisaku o hajimeta.

He threw himself into his work so he could enter a piece in the contest.

● 腰を掛ける *Koshi o kakeru*

"Sit one's hips down." Sit down, take a load off one's feet.

彼はベンチに腰を掛けて本を読んでいた。

Kare wa benchi ni koshi o kakete hon o yonde ita.

He was sitting on a bench, reading a book.

彼女はポーチに腰を掛けて空を眺めていた。

Kanojo wa pōchi ni koshi o kakete sora o nagamete ita.

She was sitting on the porch, looking up at the sky.

Also 腰掛ける *koshi-kakeru.*

尻 SHIRI
Rear, Buttocks

Shiri, often preceded by *o*, is like saying "posterior," "rear end," or "bottom." It may also be used to refer to the tail or rear end of something, as a sentence or vehicle. The man who thinks of nothing but sex, the one chasing women all the time, is said to "chase bottom" in Japanese, *onna no shiri bakari ou*.

Shiri can mean the last part of something, as in *shiri kara niban-me*, or second from the last. It may also refer to the seat of one's pants or the bottom of a pan—seen from the outside. *Ketsu*, a much less formal word for *shiri*, might best be translated as butt, buns, or ass.

● 尻が青い *Shiri ga aoi*

"Have a blue butt." [From the fact that Japanese babies have a blue spot on their butt for a short time after birth] be green, wet behind the ears.

まだ尻が青いくせに、親に対して偉そうなことを言うんじゃない。
Mada shiri ga aoi kuse ni, oya ni taishite erasō na koto o iun ja nai.
You'd better show a little more respect for your parents there, young fella.

まだ尻が青い新任社長の下では働きたくない。
Mada shiri ga aoi shinnin shachō no shita de wa hatarakitaku nai.
I'm not into working for some greenhorn that's just been kicked upstairs.

● 尻が重い *Shiri ga omoi*

"Have a heavy butt." Be slow, reluctant to start anything.

彼は尻が重くて、なかなか行動に移らない。
Kare wa shiri ga omokute, nakanaka kōdō ni utsuranai.
You'd think he had lead in his pants, slow as he is to get off his duff.

年をとるとともに、尻が重くなってきた。

Toshi o toru to tomo ni, shiri ga omoku natte kita.

The older I get, the more difficult it is for me to get started on anything.

● 尻が軽い *Shiri ga karui*

"Have a light butt." (1) [Of a woman] put out, sleep around, be an easy lay. (2) Be flighty, rash.

(1) 彼女は尻が軽い。
Kanojo wa shiri ga karui.
She puts out./ She can be had.

(2) 彼は尻が軽いので、ときどき仕事で失敗する。
Kare wa shiri ga karui no de, tokidoki shigoto de shippai suru.
He's a little flighty, so he screws things up once in a while.

● 尻に敷く *Shiri ni shiku*

"Spread on one's butt." Have someone under one's thumb; [with 〜しかれて *shikarete*] be tied to someone's apron strings.

彼は、会社ではいばっているが、家では奥さんの尻に敷かれているそうだ。
Kare wa, kaisha de wa ibatte iru ga, ie de wa okusan no shiri ni shikarete iru sō da.
He acts like he rules the roost around the office, but I hear he's henpecked at home.

彼女は結婚したらだんなを尻に敷くタイプだ。
Kanojo wa kekkon shitara danna o shiri ni shiku taipu da.
She's the type that'll want to wear the pants in the family when she gets married.

● 尻に火がつく *Shiri ni hi ga tsuku*

"A fire is lit on one's butt." Have a fire lit under one.

明日が原稿の締め切りなので、尻に火がついているのだよ。
Ashita ga genkō no shimekiri na no de, shiri ni hi ga tsuite iru no da yo.
Tomorrow's the deadline to turn in the manuscript, so I've really got to get a move on.

大都市の住宅問題は、とっくに尻に火がついているのに、解決策のないままである。

Dai-toshi no jūtaku-mondai wa, tokku ni shiri ni hi ga tsuite iru no ni, kaiketsu-saku no nai mama de aru.

The big-city housing situation has been a pressing problem for some time now, but no one has come up with a solution yet.

● 尻をぬぐう *Shiri o nuguu*

"Wipe someone's butt." Clean up after someone, clean up someone's mess.

もうこれ以上、上司の尻をぬぐうのは御免だ。

Mō kore ijō, jōshi no shiri o nuguu no wa gomen da.

I've had enough of straightening things out after the big weenies screw up.

私は幼い時から、弟の尻をぬぐってきた。

Watashi wa osanai toki kara, otōto no shiri o nugutte kita.

I've been picking up after my younger brother ever since I was a kid.

Also 尻ぬぐいをする *shiri-nugui o suru.*

● けつの穴が小さい *Ketsu no ana ga chiisai*

"Have a small asshole." Be a tightwad, stingy, a cheapskate, a piker.

開店サービスが先着5名にコーヒー半額だなんて、けつの穴が小さいなぁ。

Kaiten sābisu ga senchaku go-mei ni kōhī hangaku da nante, ketsu no ana ga chiisai nā.

Half-price coffee for the first five customers at opening! How tightfisted can you get?

けつの穴の小さい男は出世できないぞ。

Ketsu no ana no chiisai otoko wa shusse dekinai zo.

If you don't stop being such a scrooge, you're never going to get anywhere.

足 ASHI
Leg, Foot

People, dogs, insects, tables and chairs all have them. Squid have them, too. *Ashi* can be used to mean either the whole leg or just the foot, and that can lead to a lot of confusion when you're trying to figure out what's broken or where it hurts. Another meaning is mode of transportation, or more colloquially, one's wheels. So *ashi ga nai* doesn't mean that the speaker has met with some terrible accident, it just means that his car is in the shop or he has no way of getting around. *Ashi* can also mean money or "bread" when preceded by *o*, presumably because of the way it just seems to run away from you. Finally, for all you scatologists out there, the third or middle leg is the same in Japanese, *sanbon-me no ashi*.

● 足が地に着かない *Ashi ga chi ni tsukanai*

"One's feet aren't touching the ground." (1) Be extremely excited. (2) Be unrealistic, not have one's feet on the ground, impractical, have one's head up in the clouds.

(1) 3ヵ月先の旅行のことばかり考えて、足が地に着かない。
Sankagetsu-saki no ryokō no koto bakari kangaete, ashi ga chi ni tsukanai.
I feel as if I'm walking on air, the way I'm always thinking about the trip we're going on three months from now.

(2) 彼は夢ばかり追っていて足が地に着いていない。
Kare wa yume bakari otte ite ashi ga chi ni tsuite inai.
He's always up in the clouds somewhere, chasing a pipe dream.

Also 地に足が着いていない *chi ni ashi ga tsuite inai.*

● 足が出る *Ashi ga deru*

"One's feet are sticking out." Run over the budget, be in the red.

新年会で足が出た。
Shinnen-kai de ashi ga deta.
The New Year's party ran over the budget (ended up in the red).

節約したつもりだったが、今回の旅行も結局足が出てしまった。

*Setsuyaku shita tsumori datta ga, konkai no ryokō mo kekkyoku
ashi ga dete shimatta.*

I tried to keep expenses down on the recent trip but ended up in
the hole anyway.

● 足が早い *Ashi ga hayai*

"Have fast feet." (1) Be a fast runner. (2) [Of food] spoil
quickly.

(1) 彼は足が早い。
Kare wa ashi ga hayai.
He's fast on his feet. / He can really fly.

(2) 生ものは足が早いので、特に梅雨どきには注意して下さい。
*Namamono wa ashi ga hayai no de, toku ni tsuyu-doki ni wa
chūi shite kudasai.*
Fresh foods go bad quickly, so be very careful during the rainy
season.

● 足が棒になる／足を棒にする *Ashi ga bō ni naru / ashi
o bō ni suru*

"One's legs become sticks" Be so tired that one's legs feel like
rubber bands.

足が棒になるまで歩き回った。
Ashi ga bō ni naru made arukimawatta.
I walked my legs off.

足を棒にして安いアパートを探し回った。
Ashi o bō ni shite yasui apāto o sagashimawatta.
I walked around looking for a cheap apartment until I was prac-
tically dead on my feet (thought I would drop).

Now here is one that's interesting because it is similar in concept—washing something dirty off—but different in the part
of the body chosen to express the decision to turn over a new
leaf.

● 足を洗う *Ashi o arau*

"Wash one's feet." Wash one's hands of, be through with.

やくざの世界から足を洗うことにした。
Yakuza no sekai kara ashi o arau koto ni shita.
I made up my mind to go straight. / I decided to wash my hands
of the mob.

そろそろ独身生活から足を洗おうと思っている。
Sorosoro dokushin-seikatsu kara ashi o araō to omotte iru.
I think I've had just about enough of being footloose and fancy-free.

See also 手を切る *te o kiru.*

● 足を奪う *Ashi o ubau*

"Steal one's feet or legs." Strand someone, take away someone's wheels.

その電車の脱線事故は、6000人の足を奪った。
Sono densha no dassen-jiko wa, rokusen-nin no ashi o ubatta.
The train derailment left 6,000 people stranded.

大雪で、大勢の通勤客の足が奪われた。
Ōyuki de, ōzei no tsūkin-kyaku no ashi ga ubawareta.
Many commuters were left without transportation by the snowstorm.

● 足を運ぶ *Ashi o hakobu*

"Carry one's feet." Go, come, visit.

こんな田舎までわざわざ足を運んでくれて、ありがとうございます。
Konna inaka made wazawaza ashi o hakonde kurete, arigatō gozaimasu.
Thank you for coming all the way out here to the countryside to see us.

彼は情報を集めに、毎日証券会社へ足を運んだ。
Kare wa jōhō o atsume ni, mainichi shōken-gaisha e ashi o hakonda.
He went to his broker's every day to keep up on the latest developments.

Don't be tempted to use this next one like the literal English equivalent. It doesn't have anything to do with teasing anyone, but it is easy to understand why it means to hold someone back.

● 足を引っ張る *Ashi o hipparu*

"Pull someone's leg." Interfere, get in someone's way, hold someone back, cramp someone's style, skewer, hobble.

同じ職場の人間の足を引っ張るようなことはしたくない。

*Onaji shokuba no ningen no ashi o hipparu yō na koto wa
   shitaku nai.*

I don't want to stand in the way of any of my co-workers.

今回の選挙では、野党は自分で自分の足を引っ張った面もあ
る。

*Konkai no senkyo de wa, yatō wa jibun de jibun no ashi o hippat-
   ta men mo aru.*

To some extent, the opposition was its own worst enemy in the recent elections.

● 足を向ける *Ashi o mukeru*

"Point one's feet toward." (1) Go toward, head for. (2) [In the
phrase 足を向けては眠れない *ashi o mukete wa nemurenai*]
never do anything to hurt someone.

(1) 東北地方に足を向けて旅立った。

Tōhoku-chihō ni ashi o mukete tabidatta.

We set out on a trip (headed out) for the Tōhoku area.

(2) あの方に足を向けては眠れない。

Ano kata ni ashi o mukete wa nemurenai.

I could never do anything to hurt him (after all he's done for me).

● あげ足を取る *Ageashi o toru*

"Grab someone's leg when it's in the air." Pick at, trip someone
up.

彼女は、人のあげ足を取っては喜んでいる。

Kanojo wa, hito no ageashi o totte wa yorokonde iru.

She gets a kick out of finding fault with what people say.

人のあげ足ばかり取るのは、良いことではない。

Hito no ageashi bakari toru no wa, yoi koto de wa nai.

It's not right to just trip people up all the time.

● 一足違い *Hitoashi-chigai*

"One step different." Just barely.

一足違いでしたね。彼はたった今会社を出たところです。

*Hitoashi-chigai deshita ne. Kare wa tatta-ima kaisha o deta
   tokoro desu.*

You're a second too late. He just stepped out of the office.

一足違いで、彼女とすれ違いになってしまった。
Hitoashi-chigai de, kanojo to surechigai ni natte shimatta.
I just missed her by a hair.

● 二の足を踏む *Ni-no-ashi o fumu*

"Put one's second foot down." Hesitate, have misgivings.

あまりにも高くて、彼は二の足を踏んだ。
Amari ni mo takakute, kare wa ni-no-ashi o funda.
It was so expensive that he thought better of buying it.

近ごろ、彼は企業買収に対して、二の足を踏むようになった。
Chikagoro, kare wa kigyō-baishū ni taishite, ni-no-ashi o fumu yō ni natta.
He has recently come to think twice about takeovers.

ひざ HIZA
Knee

Meanings of *hiza* include both that part of the leg that kids skin all the time as well as the same part of their pants that, if not already worn through, then almost always seems to stick painfully to the wound. *Hiza* also means one's lap.

You know how when you suddenly understand something, you slap your thigh? Well, the Japanese slap their knee, *hiza o utsu*. Maybe there really *is* something to what they say about Japanese having short legs.

● ひざを突き合わせる *Hiza o tsukiawaseru*

"Shove one's knees against someone else's." (1) Sit right across from. (2) Have a friendly chat with, have a tête-à-tête.

(1) あの人と3時間もひざを突き合わせていたら、肩がこっちゃったよ。
Ano hito to san-jikan mo hiza o tsukiawasete itara, kata ga kotchatta yo.
Three hours of being holed up with him really did me in. / Boy, have I got a stiff neck after three hours of sitting shoulder to shoulder (cheek by jowl) with him.

(1) 駅周辺の再開発について、商店主たちはひざを突き合わせて話し合った。
Eki-shūhen no sai-kaihatsu ni tsuite, shōtenshu-tachi wa hiza o tsukiawasete hanashiatta.
The shop owners all got together to discuss redevelopment plans for the area around the station.

(2) 仲間とひざを突き合わせて、将来の計画を話し合った。
Nakama to hiza o tsukiawasete, shōrai no keikaku o hanashiatta.
He and his friends sat around and talked over their plans for the future.

● ひざを交える *Hiza o majieru*

"Mix knees." Get together informally.

首相は、野党の党首とひざを交えて話し合った。
Shushō wa, yatō no tōshu to hiza o majiete hanashiatta.

The prime minister had an informal chat (friendly talk) with the leaders of the opposition parties.

ひざを交えて話し合えば、彼もわかってくれるかもしれない。

Hiza o majiete hanashiaeba, kare mo wakatte kureru ka mo shirenai.

If you have a little heart-to-heart with him, he'll probably understand.

すね SUNE
Shin

The front part of the leg from the knee to the ankle is all *sune* means. Japanese college students tend to chew on their parent's shins so much, though, that you'd think there would be little left for locomotion.

● すねをかじる *Sune o kajiru*

"Chew on someone's shin." Sponge off (one's parents), be a mooch, freeload.

お前はいつまで親のすねをかじっているつもりだ。

Omae wa itsu made oya no sune o kajitte iru tsumori da.

Just how long do you think you're gonna keep mooching off your parents?

結婚後も親のすねをかじっていて、恥ずかしくないのだろうか。

Kekkon-go mo oya no sune o kajitte ite, hazukashiku nai no darō ka.

Doesn't it bother you at all to still be sponging on your parents even though you're married?

● すねに傷を持つ *Sune ni kizu o motsu*

"Have an injury on one's shin." Have a skeleton in the closet, have a (shady) past.

すねに傷を持つ身では、まともな職業にはつけないだろう。

Sune ni kizu o motsu mi de wa, matomo na shokugyō ni wa tsukenai darō.

With a skeleton in the closet like that, you're going to have trouble landing a decent job.

その飲み屋の客には、すねに傷を持つ者が多かった。

Sono nomi-ya no kyaku ni wa, sune ni kizu o motsu mono ga ōkatta.

A lot of the bar's customers had something to hide.

体 KARADA Body 身 MI Body

Except for a few instances when *mi* appears in a particular idiom, *karada* is the word you want for the physical body. *Karada* may mean either the entire body, as in *Karada ga itai* (My body aches all over), or it can mean just the trunk. *Karada* can also refer to the body as an object of sex, and one such idiom is included below. Finally, *karada* can be used when speaking of one's health, as in *Karada no guai wa ikaga desu ka*, a handy phrase to remember when you want to inquire after someone's health who has been feeling poorly.

The meanings of *mi* are more numerous than those of *karada*. In addition to the physical body, *mi* can be meat or flesh, whether human, animal, or fish. It can also mean one's person or self, as well as one's social standing or position. Lastly, *mi* is that part of the sword that slides into the scabbard, the blade.

● 体があく　*Karada ga aku*

"One's body opens." Be free.

日曜日なら体があくけれども。

Nichiyōbi nara karada ga aku keredomo.

Sunday would be fine with me. / I'll be free on Sunday.

12月は仕事に追われ、とても体のあく暇がなかった。

Jūni-gatsu wa shigoto ni oware, totemo karada no aku hima ga nakatta.

I was so busy with work in December that I didn't have any time to myself.

● 体を壊す *Karada o kowasu*

"Destroy one's body." Become ill, ruin one's health, be down.

彼女は体を壊すまで働き続けた。
Kanojo wa karada o kowasu made hatarakitsuzuketa.
She worked herself sick.

去年の夏、体を壊して2ヵ月ほど入院していました。
Kyonen no natsu, karada o kowashite ni-kagetsu hodo nyūin shite imashita.
I got sick and spent two months in the hospital last summer.

● 体を張る *Karada o haru*

"Stretch out one's body." Risk one's life, lay (put) one's life on the line, lay one's life down.

彼らは体を張って伐採に反対した。
Karera wa karada o hatte bassai ni hantai shita.
They laid their lives on the line to stop the logging operation.

体を張ってでも君を守ってみせる。
Karada o hatte de mo kimi o mamotte miseru.
I'd risk my life for you. / I'd lay down my life for you.

● 身に余る *Mi ni amaru*

"More than one's body." More than one deserves.

あなたからそのようなお言葉をいただくとは、身に余る光栄です。
Anata kara sono yō na okotoba o itadaku to wa, mi ni amaru kōei desu.
I hardly think I deserve such praise. / You are much too kind.

身に余る賞を贈られ、とても感謝しています。
Mi ni amaru shō o okurare, totemo kansha shite imasu.
I am deeply honored to be the recipient of such an award. / Thank you all so much for this most undeserved award.

● 身に覚えがある *Mi ni oboe ga aru*

"One's body remembers." Know about, have actually done something.

君にも身に覚えがあるだろう。
Kimi ni mo mi ni oboe ga aru darō.

You know what this is all about, don't you? / What I'm saying
rings a bell, doesn't it?

彼は、身に覚えのない罪で逮捕された。

Kare wa, mi ni oboe no nai tsumi de taiho sareta.

He was picked up for a crime that he knew nothing about (that
he was completely in the dark about, had nothing to do with,
hadn't committed).

● 身にしみる *Mi ni shimiru*

"Seep into one's body." (1) To the bone. (2) Be deeply impressed by something or someone, make a lasting impression
on one, sink in.

(1) 夜風が身にしみる。

Yokaze ga mi ni shimiru.

The night wind is cutting (chilling) me to the bone.

(2) 旅先での人の親切が身にしみた。

Tabisaki de no hito no shinsetsu ga mi ni shimita.

I was struck by the kindness people showed me on my trip.

● 身に付ける *Mi ni tsukeru*

"Attach to one's body." (1) Wear, put on. (2) Learn, acquire (a skill).

(1) 彼は、いつも身に付けるものに気を配っている。
Kare wa, itsu mo mi ni tsukeru mono ni ki o kubatte iru.
He pays close attention to what he wears.

(2) 再就職するために、何か技術を身につけておこうと思う。
Sai-shūshoku suru tame ni, nani ka gijutsu o mi ni tsukete okō to omou.
I'm going to learn a skill before I go back into the job market.

● 身になる *Mi ni naru*

"Become someone's body." Put oneself in someone's place.

少しは私の身になって考えてください。
Sukoshi wa watashi no mi ni natte kangaete kudasai.
Put yourself in my shoes for a minute.

親の身になって考えてみれば、そんなにわがままばかり言えないはずだ。
Oya no mi ni natte kangaete mireba, sonna ni wagamama bakari ienai hazu da.
If he ever looked at things from his parents' standpoint, he wouldn't be saying selfish things like that.

● 身を入れる *Mi o ireru*

"Put one's body into something." Throw oneself into something.

少しは勉強に身を入れなさい。
Sukoshi wa benkyō ni mi o irenasai.
It won't hurt you to study a little bit.

● 身を粉にする *Mi o ko ni suru*

"Make powder out of one's body." Work like crazy, work until one drops, bust ass, bust one's buns.

彼は借金を返すために、朝から晩まで身を粉にして働いた。
Kare wa shakkin o kaesu tame ni, asa kara ban made mi o ko ni shite hataraita.
He worked his fingers to the bone day in and day out to repay the loan.

身を粉にして働く毎日だった。

Mi o ko ni shite hataraku mainichi datta.
I was working like a dog back then.

Also 体を粉にする *karada o ko ni suru* and 身を砕く *mi o kudaku.*

Now here's a unique view of what marriage can do for you. I mean, I've always thought it was just the opposite, that people usually flab out once they're married.

● 身を固める *Mi o katameru*

"Harden one's body." (1) (Get married and) settle down. (2) Bundle up.

(1) 僕もそろそろ身を固めようと思います。
Boku mo sorosoro mi o katameyō to omoimasu.
I'm about ready to settle down and start a family myself.

(2) 防寒具に身を固めて、冬山を登った。
Bōkangu ni mi o katamete, fuyuyama o nobotta.
I bundled up in warm clothes and climbed the snowy mountain.

● 身を引く *Mi o hiku*

"Pull one's body (away)." Get out, back out; back off; retire.

社長は、来年身を引くと言っている。
Shachō wa, rainen mi o hiku to itte iru.
The president is talking about stepping down next year.

身を引く時期が来た。
Mi o hiku jiki ga kita.
The time has come to pull out.

彼女の将来を考えて、彼は身を引いた。
Kanojo no shōrai o kangaete, kare wa mi o hiita.
He decided it would be in her best interests to remove himself from the picture.

● 身を任せる *Mi o makaseru*

"Entrust one's body (to someone)." (1) Throw oneself on the mercy of someone. (2) Give oneself to someone, go to bed with a man.

(1) 運命に身を任せることにした。
Unmei ni mi o makaseru koto ni shita.

I cast my fate to the wind.

(2) その夜、彼女は彼に身を任せた。
Sono yoru, kanojo wa kare ni mi o makaseta.
She gave herself to him that night.

骨 HONE
Bone

In addition to meaning the bones that support the body of animals, birds, and fish, *hone* also can mean the framework or ribs in a fan, umbrella, *shōji*, or other man-made object. It can also refer to a person who is the heart or backbone of an organization, an essential element or aspect of something, or the quality of perserverance or spunk and hard work.

One of my favorite expressions with *hone* is *honeori-zon*—literally, breaking bones and losing. An English approximation might be something like "busting your ass for nothing."

● 骨が折れる／骨を折る *Hone ga oreru / hone o oru*

"One's bones break." Be a lot of work, not be easy, be difficult; take pains, try hard, bust ass.

この計画を彼に承諾させるのは、骨が折れるだろう。
Kono keikaku o kare ni shōdaku saseru no wa, hone ga oreru darō.
It's going to be an uphill battle trying to get him to go along with this plan.

田中さんに骨を折ってもらったおかげで、今日の会は大成功でした。
Tanaka-san ni hone o otte moratta okage de, kyō no kai wa dai-seikō deshita.
We owe the success of today's meeting to all the efforts Mr. Tanaka has made on our behalf.

● 骨を埋める *Hone o uzumeru*

"Bury one's bones." (Stay somewhere) forever, the rest of one's life.

僕は、今度の会社に骨を埋める覚悟でがんばるよ。

Boku wa, kondo no kaisha ni hone o uzumeru kakugo de ganbaru yo.

I've made up my mind to work hard and stick it out at my new job.

3年間のボランティアとして来たが、今ではこの国に骨を埋めるつもりだ。

San-nenkan no borantia toshite kita ga, ima de wa kono kuni ni hone o uzumeru tsumori da.

I came to this country as a volunteer for three years, but now I intend to be buried here.

● 骨(身)を惜しまず(惜しまない) *Hone(mi) o oshimazu (oshimanai)*

"Don't regret one's bones." Spare no pains, give something one's all, hold back nothing.

彼は骨身を惜しまず働いて、今の地位を築いた。

Kare wa honemi o oshimazu hataraite, ima no chii o kizuita.

He rose to his present position by dedicating himself entirely to the job.

骨を惜しんでいるようでは、いい職人になれないよ。

Hone o oshinde iru yō de wa, ii shokunin ni narenai yo.

You'll never make much of a craftsman if you don't put everything you've got into your work.

The next idiom appears to have its origin in the peculiar practice in Japan of the close relatives or friends of a deceased person picking up the bones after a cremation with chopsticks and transferring them to a funeral urn.

● 骨身を削る *Honemi o kezuru*

"Scrape off one's bone marrow." Toil, slave, bust ass; suffer greatly.

商家に嫁いだ祖母は、骨身を削って働いた。

Shōka ni totsuida sobo wa, honemi o kezutte hataraita.

My grandmother married into a family of merchants and worked her fingers to the bone.

あの頃は骨身を削るような生活をしていた。
Ano koro wa honemi o kezuru yō na seikatsu o shite ita.
Times were tough back then. / I used to work like a slave in those days.

血 CHI
Blood

The blood that courses through our bodies carries more than the nutrients necessary to sustain life. It is thought, poetically at least, to be an important determinant in the formation of our very nature. Idioms with *chi* are often used in describing certain strong emotions and degrees of intelligence. To be related is to "share the same blood." Beyond the realm of idioms, mates are chosen or rejected on the basis of blood type, and Japanese never seem to tire of asking one's blood type and then proceeding to explain every observed personality trait by whether one is type A, B, or O. About the only thing that even comes close to this national fascination with blood is the Western notion of zodiac signs, which, by the way, are themselves nearly as common a topic of light conversation in Japan as in the West.

● 血が騒ぐ *Chi ga sawagu*

"One's blood clamors." Get excited, (all) worked up, hopped up, hot and bothered, be hot to trot.

祭りの太鼓の音を聞いただけで血が騒いだ。
Matsuri no taiko no oto o kiita dake de chi ga sawaida.
The juices started flowing at the mere sound of the festival drums.

毎年、フットボールのシーズンになると血が騒ぐのです。
Mainen, futtobōru no shīzun ni naru to chi ga sawagu no desu.
He starts racing his motor every year when football season rolls around.

● 血の巡りが悪い *Chi no meguri ga warui*

"Have bad circulation." Be slow on the uptake, be dense.

あの人は血の巡りが悪いらしくて、つまり、ちょっと鈍いのですよ。

Ano hito wa chi no meguri ga warui rashikute, tsumari, chotto nibui no desu yo.

That guy is just a little thick, I'm afraid. / That guy's so slow—there must be something wrong upstairs.

● 血を見る *Chi o miru*

"See blood." Lead to bloodshed, come to bloodshed.

いい加減にしないと血を見るぞ。

Ii kagen ni shinai to chi o miru zo.

You're cruisin' for a bruisin', buddy. / Keep it up if you want your ass kicked.

血を見たくなければ、俺の言う通りにしろ。

Chi o mitaku nakereba, ore no iu tōri ni shiro.

Do what I say and nobody will get hurt.

最初は小さな争いだったが、とうとう血を見ることになった。

Saisho wa chiisa na arasoi datta ga, tōtō chi o miru koto ni natta.

It started out just as a little tiff, but it wasn't long before people started getting hurt.

● 血を分ける *Chi o wakeru*

"Share blood." Be related by blood, be blood relations.

あの二人は血を分けた兄弟だ。

Ano futari wa chi o waketa kyōdai da.

They're real brothers.

私に血を分けた兄がいるとは、知らなかった。

Watashi ni chi o waketa ani ga iru to wa, shiranakatta.

I never knew I had an older brother.

Also 血を引く *chi o hiku*, 血がつながっている *chi ga tsunagatte iru.*

肌 HADA
Skin

Hada derives its figurative meaning of "firsthand experience" from the fact that as a layer of cells covering the body it houses the tactile organs of sense, the nerve endings. It also has the meaning "temperament," so if your skin feels good about someone it's an indication that you can get along with that person.

An example of *kanji* giving way to *katakana*, *sukinshippu* is a late eighties coinage taken from the English words "skin" and "friendship," and indicates the bond created by physical or personal contact between humans, as between parent and child.

● 肌が合う *Hada ga au*

"Skin gets along with someone else's." Get along [usually in a negative sentence].

外国人とはどうも肌が合わない。
Gaikoku-jin to wa dō mo hada ga awanai.
I just don't seem to hit it off with foreigners.

彼女とは肌が合わない。
Kanojo to wa hada ga awanai.
I don't get along with her. / She rubs me wrong.

● 肌に合う *Hada ni au*

"Suit one's skin." Suit, be well suited for, be right for one.

このスキンクリームは私の肌に合わない。
Kono sukinkurīmu wa watashi no hada ni awanai.
This skin cream isn't right for my skin. / This isn't the right skin cream for me.

今の仕事は僕の肌に合っている。
Ima no shigoto wa boku no hada ni atte iru.
The job I have now suits me just fine. / I'm perfectly happy with my job.

● 肌で感じる *Hada de kanjiru*

"Feel something with one's skin." Experience firsthand.

雪国の冬の厳しさを肌で感じることができた。
Yukiguni no fuyu no kibishisa o hada de kanjiru koto ga dekita.
I saw firsthand just how hard winter can be in the snow country.

人々がどんなに民主主義を願っているか、肌で感じた。
Hitobito ga donna ni minshu-shugi o negatte iru ka, hada de kan-jita.
I saw for myself just how strongly people long for democracy.

● 肌を許す *Hada o yurusu*

"Allow someone to have one's skin." Give in to a man's de-mands for sex, give oneself to a man, sleep with a man.

彼女はボーイフレンドに肌を許した。
Kanojo wa bōifurendo ni hada o yurushita.
She went all the way (went to bed) with her boyfriend.

● 一肌脱ぐ *Hito-hada nugu*

"Take off a layer of skin." Help, give (lend) a helping hand, give one's right arm for someone.

彼は彼女のために一肌脱ぐことにした。
Kare wa kanojo no tame ni hito-hada nugu koto ni shita.
He decided to do what he could for her. / He made up his mind to go the extra mile for her.

彼は、その友人のためなら、一肌でも二肌でも脱ぐつもりだった。
Kare wa, sono yūjin no tame nara, hito-hada de mo futa-hada de mo nugu tsumori datta.
He was ready to give his friend the shirt off his back.

Index